# MEDICAL MYSTERIES

## SIX DEADLY CASES

# MEDICAL MYSTERIES

## SIX DEADLY CASES

BY DIAN DINCIN BUCHMAN

SCHOLASTIC INC.
New York Toronto London Auckland Sydney

ISBN 0-590-43468-3



12 11 10 9 8 7 6 5 4 3 2 1 2 3 4 5 6 7/9

Printed in the U.S.A. 28

First Scholastic printing, January 1992

# *Contents*

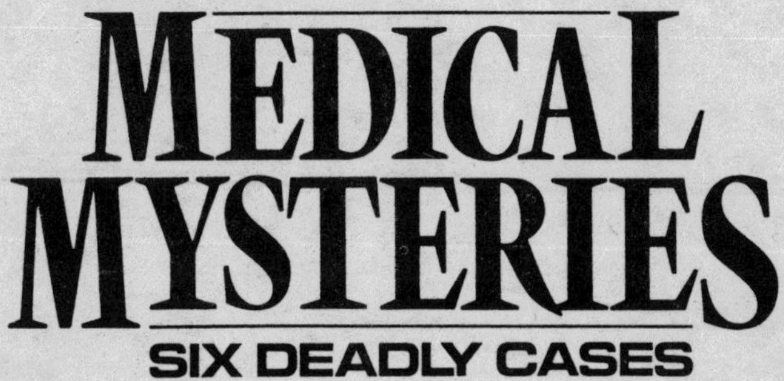
MEDICAL
MYSTERIES
SIX DEADLY CASES

# *The Moving Freckle*

*When this story began, few people had heard of the village of Lyme, Connecticut. But two mothers, and two doctors who listened to them, changed all that with an astonishing discovery. It put the word* Lyme *on everyone's lips and in the medical history books.*

In the early 1970s, Polly Murray of Lyme, Connecticut, had her first bout with an unknown illness. Sometimes she felt so tired she could barely get to her mailbox and back.

What was most puzzling about her illness was that each day she seemed to have a different complaint. Some days she was so drained of energy she felt as if she had a summer flu. Another day she had a headache, or a fever, or a bad stomachache, or her eyes would hurt. There would be strange days, even weeks, when her voice all but disappeared. The worst times were when her knees swelled up. Polly Murray was an active woman who hated not being able to walk, paint, garden, or do her housework. She was sometimes forced to hobble about on crutches. And she began to notice an odd fact: There were a lot of children in Lyme using crutches.

During this long, difficult, and painful time, no doctor could find any reason for her now-you-see-them, now-you-don't symptoms. On three particularly bad occasions, Mrs. Murray checked into the hospital for special tests. Her tests proved nothing, and the doctors shrugged off her complaints. But Polly Murray *knew* she was sick. She felt sure there was a real medical reason for her aches and tiredness.

In the fall of 1974, one of her four children, nineteen-year-old Sandy Murray, had exactly the same complaints as his mother. The next June, twelve-year-old Todd Murray's knees swelled up and he couldn't walk. He mentioned a bite. He thought that a fly had bitten his knee. Mrs. Murray's husband, Gilles, got sick that June as well. He seemed to recall a spider biting him. It was strange to see all three Murray males hobble about on crutches. The gag at the time was that it was hard to *rent* crutches in the town of Lyme.

The doctors had shrugged off Polly's complaints. Now they decided that Gilles's aches and tiredness were the result of a spider bite. One Murray son was told he had rheumatoid arthritis.

*Rheumatoid arthritis?* The athletic Murray family was devastated by the news. They learned that this serious disease of the joints could last for years and leave permanent damage. It was slight consolation to know that Gilles's troubles were only from a spider bite.

Elsewhere in Lyme, many teenage boys were waking up with knees swollen to twice their normal size. Most spent weeks in wheelchairs, recovering later with crutches. One neighborhood youngster, an eight-year-old girl, had a rash, headaches, flulike symptoms, and a facial paralysis called Bell's palsy. Other children and adults reported fast heartbeats and were told they had heart trouble.

This was a year that neighbors talked about the "annual" spring flu bug. Lots of children in Lyme had persistent sore throats and eye infections. But there are always years like that, so no one thought anything of it.

As in every small town, Polly exchanged news at the supermarket and post office. When she told neighbors that *three* people in her family were on crutches, and one had rheumatoid arthritis, they looked puzzled. Some mentioned that they knew of other Lyme children with bad joint problems — even *rheumatoid arthritis*.

A light bulb went on in Polly Murray's head.

Why were there so many local children with the same serious disease? Could juvenile arthritis be *contagious*? If it was contagious, how was it passed from one child to another? Polly Murray began to think about this problem a lot.

Not far away, in an equally attractive, heavily wooded area of Lyme, another mother, Judy Mensch, was having the same thoughts. It didn't seem too unusual when the girl next door was told she had arthritis. But by her third attack the girl was restricted to a wheelchair! Mrs. Mensch thought it odd when she heard that another girl around the corner had the same problem. And when she heard that a young boy down the block had the same symptoms, it seemed very strange.

The Mensches were very upset when their own eight-year-old daughter, Anne, became sick. Anne's knees swelled up so that she could barely walk. The family doctor diagnosed her problem as osteomyelitis and put her in the hospital. When Anne didn't get better, doctors changed the diagnosis to juvenile arthritis.

No one realized it at the time, but this very same problem was striking many families in and around Lyme. Not only in Lyme, but all over Connecticut, and in nearby Westchester County in New York. Hundreds of similar dramas were being played out on the other side of Long Island Sound, too: in Sag Harbor, Shelter Island, the Hamptons, and Fire Island. Many other states had the identical problem. The areas hit the worst at that time were Wisconsin, Minnesota, and northern California. Later, much later, it turned out that people in forty-four states had the same problems as the

Murrays and the Mensches. *There was an invisible epidemic.*

The disease was a masquerader. It had so many different symptoms that sometimes it looked like heart trouble, other times like rheumatoid arthritis. Some symptoms made it look like rheumatic fever; or lupus, a serious skin disease; or multiple sclerosis, a nerve disease. Some doctors called it viral meningitis, or other diseases with long, unpronounceable names. People with partial facial paralysis were told they had Bell's palsy.

No patient or doctor associated any of the debilitating symptoms with an earlier rash. It took two worried, fact-checking *mothers* to alert the medical profession to this important clue.

Judy Mensch had a hunch. She decided it was too much of a coincidence for four children on one street to have arthritis, so she did something about it: She called around the neighborhood to see how many people were sick. Within a few days Mrs. Mensch had gathered the names of a *dozen* other people who seemed to have recovered from, or were in the process of fighting, her daughter Anne's exact problems. She was correct in thinking it odd to have a dozen neighborhood people sick with knee inflammations.

Meanwhile, Polly Murray was also acting on a hunch. She had always felt her doctors had been wrong about her mysterious illnesses. She believed there was a reason she had been ill so often over the previous years. She became even more convinced when so many others in her family also became ill. Like Mrs. Mensch, she, too, decided to phone her neighbors for the names of people who shared the Murray symptoms. To reinforce her facts she worked out short case studies that listed the diagnosis and details.

Mrs. Murray wondered if these health problems could be due to an infection. If they were, she wanted to get help for her family and friends. In a short time, Polly Murray had a list of *thirty-five* case histories. Some were from the neighboring Connecticut villages of East Haddam and Old Lyme.

Separately, the two women piled up names and case studies. But who could they go to with the information? They both worried that local officials would laugh.

A remarkable coincidence happened next.

Judy Mensch called the Connecticut State Department of Health to talk about her list of cases. Polly Murray also called the State Department of Health with her list of case studies.

Perhaps if Connecticut were a bigger state they would each have talked to a different person. It is not unlikely that they would have been ignored. But both women spoke to the same person, Dr. David Snydman, then acting director of preventable diseases for the state of Connecticut.

Dr. Snydman was special in that he was trained by the United States Government Centers for Disease Control (called CDC) as an epidemic intelligence officer, a doctor trained to investigate any outbreak of a disease within the population. The CDC is America's disease FBI. Just as the FBI can mount a nationwide manhunt for a vicious killer or a terrorist, the CDC can provide trained disease detectives to track down an epidemic. These experts are called *epidemiologists*. An epidemiologist does not ignore warnings and suspicions of strange outbreaks; rather, he or she treats such information exactly the way a homicide detective treats a hot tip about a murder. Fortunately for Lyme and the rest of the nation, Dr. Snydman decided to investigate the Murray and Mensch stories.

This was the beginning of one of America's most unusual medical investigations.

Dr. Snydman remembers that he didn't know what he was investigating, but that it sounded interesting to him. "Both women gave me lists of names of people they thought had the same thing, and I went to work," he said.

Snydman did a thorough investigation of the facts. First he telephoned and interviewed every patient listed by Murray or Mensch. After he took their medical histories, he visited the schools they attended and then checked in with their family physicians.

Soon Snydman knew he was onto something. Everything the two women had told him was true. In this area of Connecticut there definitely was an outbreak of some kind. At first he couldn't see any common factor to link all the cases because the complaints and the symptoms were so varied. But he soon noted that almost everyone had some sort of joint inflammation. Many patients had been told they had rheumatoid arthritis. During all disease investigations, there is a pounding of the pavement, the wearing out of shoe leather as the investigator goes from person to person, door to door, to find out the facts. Sometimes there have to be smart guesses, which some people call instincts or hunches, in order for the investigation to take a big leap forward.

Such a leap now occurred. Dr. Snydman had a friend, an expert in rheumatoid arthritis: thirty-three-year-old Dr. Allen C. Steere, who had also been trained at the Centers for Disease Control. It was sheer luck that Snydman knew Steere, and sheer luck that Steere was researching rheumatoid arthritis at the Yale School of Medicine in nearby New Haven, Connecticut. Snydman decided to call Steere and tell him about his investigation. He needed Steere's feedback about the rheumatoid arthritis.

Snydman got an immediate reaction. Dr. Steere was astounded. If all these people in Lyme actually had juvenile rheumatoid arthritis, *it would be an epidemic,* and Steere had never heard of an epidemic of this kind! Steere was intrigued, and he made an unusual offer. He offered his help in getting to the bottom of the mystery. His offer would start a worldwide hunt to unravel a difficult medical mystery. Dr. Steere also got the blessings of his boss at Yale, who put the school's enormous resources behind the project.

Judy Mensch and Polly Murray were very excited by Dr. Steere's interest. At last they had found a doctor who took the symptoms seriously. Polly Murray was hopeful when Dr. Steere indicated it might even be *an entirely new disease*. If so, maybe they could find a cure. This was the first good news they'd had.

Dr. Steere was a trained epidemiologist and research scientist. He created a research plan, which he submitted to Yale's Human Investigation Committee. This insured that all work would be done with the highest research standards.

Steere could think of a hundred questions he wanted answered. Was there a link in the places people worked? Did the victims eat in the same restaurant? Had they all been to the same town picnic? Or was there a connection through the schools?

Steere called each family on the list and asked if they could help him with his investigation. Because he needed to examine, test, and talk to them, he made appointments with each family to come to his offices in New Haven. Dr. Steere received one-hundred-percent cooperation.

The list grew, and Steere soon had fifty-one families to investigate. Most patients were partially or fully recovered but twenty were ill at that time.

Dr. Steere tracked the unknown disease through the winter of 1975. At that point he called it *Lyme arthritis* (later this was changed to Lyme disease). Some cases began with a bull's-eye rash on the knee. Most had a sudden swelling in the knee that puffed the skin out several inches. Almost all of the attacks created walking problems. The muscular pains often included stiff necks and headaches. Most of the initial attacks lasted only a week, but some people had the bad luck to have attacks lasting as long as six months. The swelling and pain sometimes went away, only to return two months later. Steere didn't find any permanent damage to the patients' joints.

Many of Steere's patients had been hospitalized with severe illnesses. Some reported that their knees had been so painful they had to be drained of fluid several times. Only one of the patients had knee surgery to relieve the pain. All had been treated with old-fashioned aspirin.

Steere found an interesting clue. On four country roads near Lyme, one in every ten children had Lyme arthritis. In six of the families in the study several people were ill just like the Murrays.

Dr. Steere and his team started to eliminate the more obvious causes. One by one they checked out food, water, drugs, immunizations, schools, restaurants, and workplace possibilities. Steere found no real leads. But he did discover one thing that linked all of the patients. *They all lived in heavily wooded areas*, quite far from their neighbors.

Not one of the victims lived in the center of town.

Steere also discovered two common factors. In a quarter of the cases, people remembered the attack had started with a skin rash, usually a red bump that gradually spread into a larger ring. In addition, most of the attacks occurred between June and September. To Steere these factors strongly suggested that the disease might be related to an insect bite. If the disease seemed to break out each spring, did that mean it was caused by an insect carrying a harmful virus or bacteria?

Steere decided to check for African arboviruses, viruses transmitted by insects. He took his problem to Yale's nationally known laboratory, which deals with insect-borne viruses. If the patients had been infected by one of these viruses, they would have developed an immune reaction that would have shown up in their blood tests.

It was not an arbovirus.

With arboviruses crossed off, Steere had to consider bacteria that cause infections. But as far as he knew, all bacteria known to cause arthritis leave *permanent* joint damage, whereas this arthritis seemed to have a temporary, on-and-off pattern. Also, if the disease was caused by bacteria, traces would remain in the tissue and bloodstream of its victims. Yet every attempt to grow cultures to reveal these bacteria failed. One of the bacteria Steere tested for was rickettsia, the microbe that causes Rocky Mountain spotted fever. The test was negative.

It didn't look like bacteria was the cause of the illness. At this point Steere still suspected a virus. He put the second virus search into the hands of Yale's Dr. Warren Andiman, who checked for four different viruses.

To reveal the elusive virus, Dr. Andiman and his assistants painstakingly placed bits of tissue and fluid from the Lyme arthritis patients into individual test tubes. These were kept at body temperature. Viruses only duplicate inside living cells, so each test tube contained some animal tissue known to respond to viruses. If the cells in the tubes were infected with a virus they would change shape. Each sample was examined under a powerful microscope. The tests did not show any virus.

It was still possible that this could be a virus that nobody had ever seen before, or a virus with the ability to hide and come out later, like the herpes or chicken pox viruses. That might explain why the symptoms kept coming back.

Dr. Steere was baffled. If the disease wasn't viral and it didn't seem to be bacterial, what was it? The insect theory was tantalizing, but no one had seen any insect.

Then the invesigation took an important turn. In 1976 one of Steere's patients came in with a *new* rash. Steere had not yet seen the beginning stages of the rash. He stared at it. It was round like a bull's-eye — just as everyone had described.

Dr. Steere called everyone into the lab to have a look. He asked for a magnifying glass and peered at the rash. And then he saw it. Something — something very, very tiny — was moving a little. There was a moving *black dot, no bigger than the period at the end of this sentence*. With the huge magnifying glass Dr. Steere could see the dot was a tick. The dot was *feeding*!

Could this be the cause of Lyme arthritis?

After he took the tick out with a tweezer, Dr. Steere called in the insect specialists at Yale. What he had found turned out to be a deer tick called *Ixodes dammini*.

The tick was so very small that not one of its victims had ever noticed it. When most people go into the woods they try to avoid the larger dog or cattle tick. They hadn't noticed *Ixodes dammini* because they could hardly see it. That was why the tick could crawl for hours over someone's body, looking for a place to stay and feed. No one had even noticed the tick eating away because in its second (nymphal) stage, the tick was as small as the tiniest freckle. Who notices an extra freckle on their body? Who notices a *moving freckle* small enough to be almost invisible?

Steere found out that the deer tick has three stages in its life: In its first stage, it is as small as a period on a page. Because the bite of the tick is not painful, the bite usually goes unnoticed. Only once in a while had someone, like Todd or Gilles Murray, thought he had been bitten by a fly or a spider.

In most cases, after attaching itself, possibly

after the first twelve hours, the tick draws blood for nourishment, and then drops off after two to four days. This created a puzzle. Exactly how and why did the tick cause Lyme arthritis? Was it possible that it wasn't the tick itself, but something living inside the tick that caused the damage?

This was a good guess, but it would take years and years of painstaking laboratory investigation to find the answer to this important question. The job was assigned to a top Montana microbiologist, Dr. Willy Burgdorfer of the Rocky Mountain Laboratories at the Centers for Disease Control. By 1982 Dr. Burgdorfer was able to isolate a very tiny corkscrew-shaped bacterium that sometimes (but not always) lives inside the deer tick. *Not all deer ticks are infected.* The corkscrew-shaped bacterium is called a spirochete. This particular bacterium was then named in honor of Dr. Burgdorfer and is called *Borrelia burgdorferi*.

Dr. Burgdorfer discovered that when an infected tick lands on a person (or on any other animal or a bird) after about twelve hours it feeds for twelve to twenty-four hours. *If* the tick is infected, twelve to twenty-four hours elapse before the infection is transmitted. During this time, the spirochete — the corkscrew-shaped bacterium — is deposited and moves into any nearby capillary vein. This spirochete causes the symptoms of Lyme disease by traveling through the bloodstream, and invading various organs of the body.

We now know that Lyme disease exists on all

continents except Antarctica. In the United States it can be found in forty-four states. The highest concentrations of Lyme disease are in the northeast, the upper Midwest, and along the northern California coast. About ninety percent of the cases are in eight states: New York, Connecticut, California, Massachusetts, Minnesota, New Jersey, Rhode Island, and Wisconsin.

Lyme disease can be found in Europe, especially in Germany and the Scandinavian countries. It also exists in China and the Soviet Union. Cases have been traced to Europe as far back as 1900, so epidemiologists now think it is possible that the corkscrew spirochete was brought here by birds flying from one continent to another. These migratory birds may also be the cause of the rapid spread of Lyme disease from one area to another, and may account for its rapid spread in the United States.

People of any age can get Lyme disease. Those who spend time outdoors in tick-infested environments are at an increased risk of exposure. Most victims have reported an exposure to ticks or their woodland brush habitat during June, July, and August, but cases have been reported during every month of the year.

Even now, when we know so much about Lyme disease, most of the people bitten by the tiny tick never even realize they have been bitten unless they get a rash. The bull's-eye rash can appear from two days to five weeks after a person is bitten.

Seventy-five percent of those bitten do get a rash. But that means twenty-five percent may have no warning.

With each passing summer, Lyme disease has become an increasing concern. No one knows why the *Ixodes* tick and the Lyme bacterium have spread so rapidly. Unfortunately, any contact with grass or leaves, even just walking through a park, is enough for a tick to attack a host. Every summer there are thousands of cases reported. Now most experts believe that most of the cases go undetected, misdiagnosed, or unreported to health officials. Some experts think the number of cases may be as many as 20,000 a year or higher. And the disease is spreading fast.

Lyme disease is spread by a bacterium that is part of the natural cycle of deer ticks feeding on animals such as mice, possums, dogs, or deer. At certain stages, the tick, especially the nymph, can feed on a human, and *if* the tick is infected with the bacterium, can cause an infection in people. Cases of Lyme disease have also been reported in dogs, horses, and cattle. The good news is: *No person can spread Lyme disease to another person.*

Although the *Ixodes dammini* are called deer ticks, it appears that deer are not the principal carrier of the bacteria, though they can become infected. In the eastern United States white-footed field mice serve as the main hosts for both the bacteria and the young ticks. In the West, the main hosts are lizards and jackrabbits. But white-tailed deer are necessary for the survival of the *adult* ticks.

The nymphs, or young ticks, are the chief threat to humans. About seventy percent to ninety percent of all cases are caused by nymph bites. Adult ticks are generally less of a threat to humans because the adults are large enough to be seen and removed before they can transfer the bacteria. Removal within three hours greatly reduces the risk of infection.

How do the ticks find animal hosts since they can't fly or jump? They wait. They can wait for long periods in low vegetation in wooded areas and grasslands and transfer themselves to whatever, or whoever, brushes by. Often dogs and cats carry ticks to people's homes and property.

Investigators have discovered that Lyme disease usually occurs during the summer months and generally starts within a month of exposure to an infected tick. The circular, reddish, expanding rash may come out in several places. During the rash stage, or occasionally just before the rash shows up, other symptoms such as fever, headache, fatigue, stiff neck, muscle and/or joint pain may be present. These may last several weeks. If left untreated, within a few weeks to months after the rash comes out complications such as meningitis, facial palsy, or heart abnormalities may occur. Swelling and pain in the large joints may recur over many years. A past infection with Lyme disease does not seem to make a person immune.

Several patients have been reinfected.

The current therapy includes the use of tetracycline or penicillin.

Fortunately, this tick-borne disease is treatable and curable during its early stages when only rash and flulike symptoms are present. Early treatment is crucial; it reduces the possibilities of complications and increases the chance of cure. If antibiotics are prescribed immediately, most patients recover completely.

# *The Mystery of the Poisoned Boys*

*No one knew it at first, but the boy had been poisoned. His teacher was the first to notice his sudden change from a smiling, enthusiastic boy to a frightened, lifeless child. She asked the principal to call his mother* immediately *to take him home. This was just the beginning of a frightening medical mystery.*

**M**iguel (that is not his real name) only seemed a little sick when his mother, Maria, took him to the doctor. Because the doctor didn't see anything wrong he sent Miguel back home to rest. The doctor was completely surprised when the Torreses were back in his office an hour later. Miguel's mother was in a panic. The doctor could now understand why. There had been abrupt and dangerous changes in eight-year-old Miguel Torres. His skin looked washed out. He couldn't open his eyes, his body was limp, and his muscles were twitching. His heartbeat was uneven. He felt sick to his stomach.

Suddenly Miguel had diarrhea. Then he vomited. Even more suddenly he was cold and senseless — almost unconscious. Knowing no logical reason for the rapid disintegration of Miguel's health, the doctor telephoned a leading Fresno pediatrician, Dr. John P. Conrad, Jr., an expert in children's diseases.

Dr. Conrad, who was associated with a hospital that worked only with children, realized that this case was *urgent*. He telephoned ahead to the Children's Hospital and ordered a blood test to check for diabetes. When Miguel and his mother arrived, everything was ready. The tests were finished by the time Dr. Conrad dashed in. The blood test didn't show diabetes. But there was an alarming problem with Miguel's white blood cell count. It was abnormally high. Why?

Miguel's skin was not only very pale, but now it was also cold and clammy. His heart was racing, and the muscles of his hands and feet were twitching. Dr. Conrad noted a new and important symptom. The pupils of Miguel's eyes had narrowed to tiny specks. The pain in his stomach area was so bad he screamed when the doctor touched him lightly during the examination.

Dr. Conrad stared at Miguel. Whatever was wrong with the boy had obviously gotten worse.

What could it be? Was it bacteria that caused his violent diarrhea? Dr. Conrad tested for shigella, a bacterium that causes diarrhea. But the test came back negative.

Dr. Conrad had a hunch chemical poisoning was causing the damage. The symptoms pointed that way. He ran Miguel's symptoms through his mind. Miguel was acting strangely. He looked lifeless, and he had a terrible stomachache. His pupils were almost invisible.

What kind of poisoning could it be? To Dr. Conrad's practiced eye, Miguel's acute illness looked as if it could be a reaction to an organic phosphate. Fresno is a big industrial farming area. The farmers were always spraying chemicals to kill insects. Perhaps Miguel had inhaled some toxic insecticide from a crop duster or local farm sprayer.

Dr. Conrad needed some leads. Mrs. Torres hesitantly told him that Miguel had mentioned seeing a spray machine and a spray plane that morning on the way to school. Dr. Conrad knew that organic phosphates are dangerous and can penetrate the skin. The symptoms do show up in a few hours.

The facts weren't all in yet, but because of Miguel's condition and the possibility of it being a spray, the doctor decided to treat the case as if it were caused by an organic phosphate. He had no other ideas.

Dr. Conrad had to accomplish three things to help Miguel survive while he tried to solve the mystery.

First Dr. Conrad had to replace the fluids that Miguel had lost with his violent vomiting and diarrhea. Dr. Conrad ordered intravenous fluids to be dripped into Miguel's vein. The doctor's next job was to fight against the poison in Miguel's body. He had previous experience with chemical poisoning and had used the lifesaving drug atropine with good effect. Finally Dr. Conrad needed to *extract* the poison, but he couldn't do that until he knew which poison it was. In order to find that out he needed accurate blood tests. At eight-thirty that night he had the blood tests back. It *was* organic phosphate poisoning. He had made the right guess.

The emergency staff at Valley Children's Hospital were now checking Miguel every few minutes. The drug Dr. Conrad had chosen was working like a charm. If it hadn't, the doctor would have had to use an even more powerful drug. But everything was going so well Conrad decided he didn't need to. By ten o'clock Miguel's condition had stabilized. Dr. Conrad was satisfied and went home.

Miguel continued to do well on the fluids and the atropine for several days. In the meantime, the local sprayers were questioned. Their answers surprised Dr. Conrad. They had *not* used organic phosphate on the crops. This was a puzzle! Where then did Miguel pick up the organic phosphate poisoning?

After six days in the hospital Dr. Conrad was delighted to see Miguel in his private office, well and back to his normal self. The doctor sent Miguel home to rest for an entire week. Dr. Conrad examined his next two patients. His office nurse interrupted him with an emergency. Mrs. Torres was back in the office, and she was in a panic. Miguel was sick again! He was so sick he couldn't get out of the car.

Dr. Conrad rushed out to the parking lot. Miguel was now sweating and breathing hard. He was in a state of shock. He couldn't move his legs. Maria Torres explained that Miguel had gotten sick almost as soon as they had left the doctor's office. She had turned the car around and raced back to the doctor. Dr. Conrad jumped into the car and told Mrs. Torres to drive back to the hospital as fast as she could.

All this seemed like a nightmare to Dr. Conrad. The case was repeating itself, only this time Miguel appeared to be even sicker than before. Miguel's violent cramps began again. He began to vomit. Dr. Conrad repeated his first prescriptions: fluids, and the antipoison drug atropine. Because the boy seemed in so much danger, he also added a more powerful drug.

Luckily Mrs. Torres had had the presence of mind to turn her car around and come back to the doctor's office. This was a matter of life and death. The doctor and the nurses hovered around Miguel for the next few hours, and then slowly, slowly they saw some small improvement. Miguel would *live*. Dr. Conrad and the staff were ecstatic.

By the next morning, Miguel stabilized. Everyone agreed he had made an unusual and remarkable recovery.

Now there was time to stop and think about the cause of Miguel's strange illness. If Miguel had been poisoned somehow, and it hadn't been by a crop sprayer, how had he picked up the poison?

Conrad called the Fresno County Public Health Department the next morning and told them the facts of the case. Miguel had recovered and was doing well after a week at home, but he had then become critically ill one hour after seeing the doctor. Conrad asked for help in tracking down the source of the organic phosphate poison. Because the last episode happened in the car, maybe it was the Torres' car. Dr. Conrad also advised the health department that they should check everything the boy was wearing: The problem might be with his clothes.

An investigator and an assistant were sent out immediately. Soon they were talking with Mrs. Torres, checking for sprays around the house, garage, and car.

They checked to see if there was a garden spray or insecticide bomb. No. Did the family have phosphates in the garage, laundry area, or kitchen? No. What about Miguel's clothes? Mrs. Torres showed them the blue jeans and shirt Miguel had worn that day.

There was a store label on the blue jeans. They asked Mrs. Torres if she had bought the jeans at that store. Her answer interested them. She had not bought them at a store, but had found them at a salvage sale at a local trucking company. She told them the jeans had looked perfect when she bought them, and they were so cheap she bought five pairs.

They asked if her son had worn all five pairs. "No," she answered, "only one."

Actually, Miguel had worn this same pair two times. He wore them to school the day he got sick. And he had put them on again when he left the hospital, the day he saw the doctor.

The investigators couldn't contain their excitement. This had to be the answer! Miguel had been wearing the jeans both times when he had become so violently ill. It *had* to be the jeans.

To be absolutely sure, the health department workers decided to give the jeans a mosquito test. They carefully wrapped the five pairs of jeans and took them to the state health department laboratory. Here lab technicians put the jeans in the cage of one of the mosquito colonies they were breeding. Then they all watched in fascination. Fifteen minutes later, *every mosquito in that colony had died*. Strangely enough, a nearby colony in the lab died five minutes later. The second colony hadn't even had direct exposure to the jeans. The poison in the jeans was *deadly*.

Now the health department needed to find out three things: the product name of the poison (there are about twenty-five commercial phosphates sold in the United States); how many jeans had been contaminated by the poison; and the names of any other people who had bought jeans at the sale. Other children could get sick, too.

At that very moment, something else was happening at the Fresno General Hospital. As Dr. Conrad was making the rounds of young patients with the resident and interns, he shared with them the entire story of Miguel and his poisoned pants. This turned out to be a lucky coincidence for another eight-year-old.

The very next day, the chief resident telephoned Dr. Conrad for some advice. The resident had a young patient (whom we shall call Jimmy) who had come into the hospital with many of the same symptoms as Miguel.

Jimmy had been vomiting, and he was dizzy and sweating. Like Miguel, when he was admitted to the hospital he seemed almost unconscious, and his pupils were so small you could hardly see them. The boy was also twitching and had severe cramps. Jimmy's own doctor was puzzled by these symptoms and at that time thought it might be acute rheumatic fever. But the resident had just heard the story of Miguel, and Jimmy's symptoms matched. He asked Dr. Conrad if he could test the boy for organic phosphate poisoning. The resident and Dr. Conrad together ordered the test that would reveal any poison.

The results came back in a few hours. The resident was right. The second boy was also poisoned by an organic phosphate. Now they would have to find out if this boy had the same kind of salvage-sale jeans. They checked with the boy's mother. Sure enough, the boy had been wearing a *new pair of jeans*. They, too, had been bought at a salvage sale.

The story was practically the same. Jimmy had worn the jeans to school and had become so sick the school had sent him home. He recovered slowly at home for a few days and then went back to school. Like Miguel, Jimmy had put on the same pair of jeans. Immediately afterward he had been rushed to the Fresno General Hospital, violently ill. Fortunately for Jimmy, the resident had remembered and acted upon the unusual story Dr. Conrad had shared the day before.

Now there wasn't another moment to waste. The rest of the jeans had to be tracked down. Miguel's mother had bought five. This new pair made six. But how many other pairs were there in that salvage sale? The trucking company refused to cooperate, and said they didn't know the answers. The health department called all the local newspapers and the television and radio stations. They issued an urgent call: DID YOU BUY JEANS AT A SALVAGE SALE? THEY ARE DANGEROUS. BRING IN THOSE JEANS!

Four more pairs of jeans were returned to the health department. Later, the health department would find out there were only ten pairs in all. Of the four additional pairs returned, two had been worn. Strangely, the boys who wore these jeans never got sick. That small mystery was soon solved with a simple one-word answer: *WASHING*. The two pairs of jeans had been washed before the boys wore them. The washing had eliminated all of the poison.

Tracing how the jeans had been contaminated proved to be a more difficult task. Eventually the health department learned that the jeans had been shipped in a giant truck with both machinery and chemicals. No one knew how, but one five-gallon can of organic phosphate had leaked. This leak soaked ten pairs of jeans. The jeans shipment had stayed in a warehouse for some time, where the jeans dried, and the visible stain from the chemical disappeared. However, when the jean order was delivered, the store didn't think the trousers looked fresh and clean. They returned the jeans to the trucking company. The jeans were then put into a distress sale at the trucking depot. Two mothers almost lost their sons.

# *The Hidden Time Bomb*

*Love Canal is the name of a place near Niagara Falls, New York. Today these two words are synonymous with pollution. Not ordinary, everyday pollution, but the kind that is life-threatening. This is a tale of people who unknowingly lived above a poisonous dump of rotting chemicals.*

This story begins quite innocently about 100 years ago, when a New York businessman, William Love, started to build a canal. The canal was part of his dream to help produce cheap electric power. When the canal was one mile long, fifteen yards wide, and forty feet deep, Love ran out of money. The abandoned ditch was soon filled by springs and streams and rainwater, and it soon became a favorite swimming hole in the summer, and skating pond in the winter for the people who lived nearby. Years later the county used the drained ditch for a garbage dump.

Niagara County, where Love Canal is located, is a big chemical production center, and soon the ditch became valuable property. In 1942 it was sold to a local chemical manufacturing company. The Hooker Chemical Company bought the old canal to use as a dump site for its chemical trash.

This was the beginning of a nightmare that would eventually affect 200 families living right next to the canal, and a second ring of families, living just a little farther away. All in all, as many as 1,000 families would be affected.

When the Hooker Chemical Company was filling in its dump in the 1940s, there were no local or federal laws to control hazardous waste materials. For ten years or so, day after day, year after year, Hooker Chemical Company trucks dumped tons of chemical waste into the canal, over 21,800 tons in all. The waste included over *200* different chemical compounds, some of which were among the most dangerous substances ever invented. Many were known to cause cancer and produce birth defects. Dioxin, part of Agent Orange, a lethal chemical used in the Vietnam War, was one such chemical. Benzene, which can cause leukemia, was another. The list was long.

In 1953, Hooker decided to abandon its chemical trash dump. Hooker claims, but cannot prove, that the chemicals were covered with clay to prevent leakage before the canal was filled with dirt. Nature has a wonderful way of renewing itself, and the area was soon covered with sapling trees, plants, and wildflowers. In a short time the former canal looked like any other filled-in land. In the surrounding area there were enough local farmlands, apple and peach orchards, sparkling brooks, and woods filled with deer and birds to make the old Love Canal dump invisible, and its name forgotten.

In the 1950s local Niagara County land was still cheap. Developers bought acreage near the old Love Canal and built hundreds of houses for returning World War II veterans and their wives. Nearby, low-income federal housing was built as well. Oddly, the entire new neighborhood was given the same sequence of street numbers as another Niagara Falls neighborhood. The development company never built the grand park it promised, nor the playground.

Where there are young families, there is a need for a school. The local Niagara Falls Board of Education began to look for an inexpensive site for an elementary school. They didn't have to look long. Hooker Chemical Company donated the old canal land to the board. All Hooker asked for was *one dollar*, and a signed deed for the property. In exchange for that dollar Hooker demanded that it never be blamed for any lawsuit, damage, injury, or death resulting from any of the waste materials buried in the canal.

In 1955 the board built an elementary school on

the corner of the old canal, which was now called 99th Street. Since there was no playground, the children played in the nearby empty lot. Many children also played in and around the nearby creek. Some families would soon have a great reason to regret this.

On the surface, the neighborhood looked like a suburban paradise. There were fine new houses with front and backyards, and only a short walk to a brand-new elementary school. Unlike most suburbs there were woods to play in, and streams to wade in. Some people could even fish at the edge of their own property. What more could you ask for?

The neighborhood's mysterious troubles happened slowly. At first the troubles were so simple and personal that each family thought only they were the ones having bad luck. No one connected their troubles to anyone else's or to neighborhood problems. Of course, at that time, everyone thought they were living on old *farmland*. No one realized they were living over a poisonous dump. No one remembered the name: Love Canal.

When they moved in during the 1950s and after, some of the home owners could not grow any grass. The unlucky home owners who had unknowingly moved to the streets next to the old canal kept trying to grow plants, bushes, trees, and flowers, but most of their plants withered.

Among the early troubles were rashes that appeared as soon as people moved to the area. It seemed that for as long as anyone could remember, someone was always complaining about an irritating rash. But the truly terrifying rashes took a long time to show up. One of the worst rash episodes occurred in the 1970s to Rosalee Janese. She had tried to clean up the black sludge oozing out of the drain of her swimming pool. Soon afterward she had pimples and sores *over her entire body*. They would not go away.

Another problem didn't appear immediately but after about ten years. Around 1962, some people started complaining about the noxious chemical smells in the area. Where could these smells have come from, when the whole area had had a sweet "country" smell when they moved in?

Gradually, people on certain streets noticed smells coming from their basements. They were puzzled, but very few complained about it to their neighbors.

One reason people didn't talk much about the smells is that Niagara County is a manufacturing and chemical center. Many young home owners in the area worked for one of the big plants. No one wanted to interfere with their pension rights from the factories. It was understood that the bad chemical smells were part of the price they paid for living in such an active industrial area. Most people thought the smells were actually from the nearby factories.

Pat and Peter Bulka moved to 97th Street in 1965. They had seven children and thought the quiet LaSalle neighborhood would be a great place to raise a family. There was a big empty lot next to their backyard. When the Bulkas bought the house, the real-estate agent told them a park was planned for that nearby lot. (It was never built.)

In the spring of 1966 Pat looked out her window and saw that her eldest son, John, and his three-year-old brother, Joey, were in the side yard happily fishing for tadpoles in a shallow gully filled with spring rain. Satisfied that they were safe, she had walked into her living room when she heard them screaming. She ran outside. Joey had fallen into the puddle, and his big brother John had dived in to rescue him. Both were now standing by the ditch. *Both were covered from head to toe with a black, oily slime.*

Pat wondered how the slime had gotten there — the ditch seemed to be filled with ordinary rainwater! It was scary. Pat Bulka had to throw the clothes away, and it took two or three weeks of frequent scrubbing before the two boys smelled clean again. Joey developed chronic ear problems after he slipped into the muck. Two of his sisters also developed ear problems. John Bulka began to have chronic respiratory ailments by the year he entered eighth grade.

After the black-slime incident, Pat and Peter Bulka called the local health department to complain. The department took samples from the gully, but insisted nothing was wrong. Oddly, the Bulkas' complaints annoyed many of their neighbors, and as a result some didn't talk to them for a long time afterward. Neighborhood people didn't want their property values to go down.

During the years from 1966 to 1978 the following things happened in the LaSalle neighborhood on or near the old Love Canal:

No one said anything when, after a rainstorm, fields in back of people's houses filled up with chemical-smelling black ooze. The slime smelled just like the odor from the factories up the Niagara River.

Almost everyone complained of headaches.

People wondered why their hair came out in clumps when they combed and brushed it.

So many people became hard of hearing that they began to sadly joke that it must be contagious. Here and there babies were born deaf. On one street there were so many deaf children that a sign was put up reading: CAUTION: DEAF CHILD AREA.

Everyone knew young women who were having trouble bearing healthy babies. Many of the women in the neighborhood had frequent miscarriages.

How does a lifetime of living on a poisonous dump change your life? A disaster was ticking away underneath these families like a time bomb. Not until much later would they figure out that the storm sewers under the ground, the old moist marshes called swales, and the underground artesian wells and springs all played a part in making Love Canal a treacherous place to live. When the barrels in which the hazardous chemicals were buried started to rust and rot and the chemicals leaked, the sandy soil, underground streams, and marshes underneath all contributed to the slow, steady flow of the chemicals away from the dump and into the land beneath the homes in the area.

At that time no one knew that the worst problems would be for those who lived nearest to the old canal: nearest to the school and the chemical dump site.

John Kerr was an electrician at the Union Carbide plant. He, his wife, Christine, and their children, Deborah and Matthew, lived on a street next to the old canal. The Kerrs were heartsick because Deborah had an "old person's disease," rheumatoid arthritis, and was plagued with kidney and bladder infections. There was even more trouble with Matthew. He had a rare heart disease, permanent damage to his legs, and a learning disability.

The Schroeders, who lived on the very edge of the old canal, also had terrible health problems. The mother, Karen, complained of agonizing headaches. The father, Tim, bought an old bulldozer to lift the black gook that was oozing into their backyard. Tim had the same trouble most people had who were living back-to-back with the old canal. As soon as they touched the slimy ooze, they got a rash. Sometimes the rash wasn't confined to their hands and popped up on other parts of their bodies. But Tim developed an embarrassing new problem right after his rash appeared. He could hardly stay awake.

The Schroeders were also upset about the health of their daughters. Little Lauri seemed to be losing her hair. Sheri was born mildly retarded. She also had a cleft palate and two sets of bottom teeth.

Joanne and Gary Hale also had two daughters. Joanne and Gary both had troubles with hip tumors. Gary had one tumor removed. Joanne had two removed and spent six months at a time in a wheelchair. Daughter Lisa was born with birth defects, and then suddenly, "for no known reason," the doctor said, one of her legs stopped growing! Their other daughter, Carrie Ann, was only two years old when the grief-stricken Hales were told her poor health was due to "a failure to thrive."

Carrie Ann also had a weird thing happen to her teeth. When she was three years old, all of her baby teeth fell out but no new teeth grew back.

To Joanne it seemed that whenever the family solved one problem, another one came up. "They kept coming back and coming back. All we could do was sit and wait for the next thing to happen," she recalls about that time in her life.

Pat Brown's daughter developed a cancerous growth on her knee, and for a long time the little girl couldn't straighten out her legs. The youngster spent a lot of time either in a wheelchair or on crutches.

Barb and Jim Quimby were joyous at the birth of their child, Brandy, in 1972. Unfortunately, Brandy was retarded.

All these things and more were happening from 1953 until 1978 when a newspaper story in the *Niagara Gazette* hit the area like a bombshell. An investigative reporter, Mike Brown, wrote a series of articles about the area called Love Canal. He named the streets that were built on top of and near the old Love Canal. Because there were two neighborhoods in Niagara Falls with the same street numbers, and no one had ever heard the words Love Canal before, each neighborhood thought it was the other neighborhood — at first.

Lois Gibbs, the wife of a chemical worker, Harry Gibbs, lived on 101st Street. Michael, her son, had had epileptic seizures as soon as he started school. Lois Gibbs read every word of the articles. When she read that the chemicals dumped into the canal could cause seizures, she wondered if her son's seizures could have been caused by the chemicals.

Wondering is usually the beginning of figuring things out.

Could there be a connection between Michael Gibbs's illness and the old chemical dump? In case there was a connection, Lois Gibbs asked the principal if she could transfer Michael to another school. The principal said no. Lois was outraged, and decided to take a petition about the transfer to her neighbors.

Lois Gibbs went from house to house with the

petition about her son, and discovered what few people in the neighborhood knew. She was horrified when she got a complete overview of the health of her neighbors. They were *all* worried and sick! Lois Gibbs and others soon found that their neighborhood had "geographic" groups of illnesses. These clusters of illnesses corresponded to the underground marshes. Because the marshes had no definite or regular shape, the pattern of each illness was not obvious. Much later, scientists theorized that each marshy swale had a more or less separate chemical character. One swale absorbed a chemical that seemed to cause deafness. Another swale seemed to absorb chemicals that caused birth defects. Yet another swale absorbed a chemical that seemed to cause cancer.

Lois Gibbs was in a state of shock as she went from door to door and discovered the truth about the health of her neighbors. People were relieved to share their troubles and fears with her. She slowly discovered who had cancer and who had already died of cancer. Her neighbors told her of their many odd and recurring rashes. And she learned which of them were hard of hearing and which were deaf. Many young married women complained they couldn't get pregnant. She was horrified to learn how many of her neighbors had even more devastating problems. Many of the neighborhood children had been born with birth defects.

To Lois Gibbs and others, it became clear that

this neighborhood was not normal, and Lois Gibbs began to make a list. Outraged at the extent of the tragedy, Gibbs sought out her neighbors and organized a local home-owners association. She became an activist and an organizer. But Lois Gibbs was not the only one. Love Canal developed many activists as people learned that they had to fight.

Love Canal was the *first* of many pollution scandals in the United States. The mystery of the illnesses, and the horrifying effects of the hidden chemicals, shocked the entire world. Now the name Love Canal has instant recognition — Love Canal means pollution. Pollution that poisons life and health and happiness.

As the mysteries were uncovered, and the danger to children, born and unborn, was presented, the New York State Health Department became involved. That is why on August 2, 1978, it investigated the entire area and declared a health emergency for all homes bordering the canal.

By August 7th, 1978, the news about people's health was so bad that President Carter declared Love Canal a limited disaster area. That month, 238 frightened families, those whose houses bordered the canal, were evacuated and relocated. These 238 homes, purchased by the state, were later torn down. The land that these houses stood on will never be used again.

But then there was the question of their neighbors. Families outside the circle of the 238 nearest to the canal became frightened and alarmed about their own health and future. They, too, felt their lives were in jeopardy. Nearly two years later, after frantic petitioning and a national uproar, on May 22, 1980, President Carter declared a federal emergency that covered six more blocks from the center of the canal. About 400 more families were evacuated, and their homes were bought with state and federal funds. All in all, more than 2,500 residents left Love Canal during the evacuations. Oddly, sixty Love Canal families refused to leave their homes! They continued to live in their houses on the mostly abandoned streets.

However, most of the former Love Canal residents decided it was not enough to get money merely for their contaminated homes and land. They would need money to pay for care for their continuing health problems. The former Love Canal residents were finally awarded a total of twenty million dollars. In 1986, the residents of the old Love Canal, the most famous polluted homesite in America, lined up outside a Niagara Falls bank to receive their share of the settlement.

At that time Marie Pozniak, who has had several cancer operations and who has a daughter born with several birth defects, said, "They could give me the whole twenty million and it wouldn't compensate me for the mental anguish I face every time I look at my daughter." Mrs. Pozniak fears all of her daughters may have genetic damage.

Many former residents have exactly the same fears: They worry that the old poisoned ground they lived on will leave a terrible legacy. They worry that even their children's children will be scarred by the deadly chemicals from Love Canal.

# *The Twin Who Didn't Get Sick*

*"If I had only known the exact questions to ask," the disease detective recalls many years later, "I might have solved the case right then and there! But then nobody knows the exact questions to ask until a pattern is found."*

*It was the twin who* didn't *get sick who held the missing clue to the case.*

In the spring of 1968 the five doctors in West Branch, a small city of 10,000 people near the north woods of Michigan, knew they had a serious epidemic on their hands.

Twenty kids and grown-ups had the same set of symptoms: high fever, nausea, vomiting, tiredness, and no desire to eat. Each and every patient's skin became yellowed, and their urine was very dark.

This was not the flu. It could only be acute viral hepatitis — a highly infectious disease, easily spread from one patient to another. Hepatitis demands strict hygiene and bedrest, so most of the West Branch patients were sent to the hospital.

Viral heptatitis spreads so rapidly that it must be reported to local health officials. All five doctors quickly passed this news on to the district health officer, Dr. Ophelia Baker. One of the doctors, happened to be her husband, Dr. Thomas Baker.

On hearing the news, Dr. Ophelia Baker immediately checked past district-health records. What was West Branch's normal caseload for hepatitis? What was the record for the past year, 1967? In the entire year of 1967 there had only been seven cases. Now there were twenty in the space of a few days. This was only the beginning. New cases were cropping up *by the hour*. This was an epidemic. Dr. Baker knew that in the race against hepatitis, time is the important factor, so she promptly reported the epidemic to the Michigan State Department of Health.

Dr. Baker made two urgent requests: One was for large amounts of gamma globulin to inoculate anyone who had any contact with a hepatitis victim. To accomplish this she had to mount a huge campaign that would include the families, school friends, teachers, and business associates of each victim. Gamma globulin, now called immune globulins, are sterile solutions of antibodies from human (blood) plasma. Injecting the population in West Branch and the surrounding areas would give each person about a week's immunity to the disease. Dr. Baker was gambling that she could control the epidemic within this time frame.

Because she was racing against time, Dr. Baker knew she had to find the *source* of the infection, and quickly, too. Acute viral hepatitis generally comes from a specific source. Likely sources could be contaminated milk, shellfish, water, or fruit. Or one or more *persons* could be passing on the disease. In the beginning stage of viral hepatitis any patient who handles food, milk, water, or fruit for other people could transmit the disease. That is why every patient with the disease was told to wash his or her hands after going to the bathroom. Whatever the cause, Dr. Baker knew it was urgent to track down the thing or person or persons who were responsible for this outbreak, otherwise the epidemic would multiply even faster.

Because Dr. Baker knew she would be totally involved in the inoculation program, her second request to the state health department was to ask the Centers for Disease Control in Atlanta, Georgia, for an epidemiologist: a trained epidemic hunter. She had some guesses about the possible cause of this epidemic, but she didn't want to guess. She needed to know the facts.

In the meantime, Baker's job was to prevent the epidemic from spreading. Not only was prevention important for every resident of this northern Michigan rural area, but since this was spring, within days and weeks thousands of vacationers were expected to open their fishing, hunting, and vacation homes. Dr. Baker knew she would have to protect these incoming vacationers by finding and eliminating the common source of the viral infection.

Dr. Baker and the other physicians in the town started a mass inoculation program. Within two weeks they had inoculated all known contacts of the victims — as many as 7,000 people!

There was bad news, though — still more patients were cropping up every day. The epidemic had started April 30. By May 17 the list of hepatitis patients included *thirty-two* grownups and children, most of them teenagers. That was the day Dr. Baker requested help from the Centers for Disease Control.

The CDC called on Dr. Stephen Schoenbaum, a gifted twenty-six-year-old epidemic intelligence officer working in Atlanta.

When he drove up to the Bakers' house in his rented Ford, Dr. Ophelia Baker greeted him at the door. Her husband, Dr. Thomas Baker, and the big Baker Clan all welcomed Dr. Schoenbaum as if they had known him all their lives. They invited him to join them for dinner. The Bakers' hospitality was irresistible, and the Baker home became Schoenbaum's headquarters.

Dr. Baker told Schoenbaum the number of cases had increased from thirty-two to thirty-nine in the last two days. Most of the patients had been sick enough to need hospitalization. She gave him the basic facts on each patient: name, address, age, and sex. She mentioned that in early April there had been another tiny, short-lived epidemic of hepatitis.

At first glance Dr. Schoenbaum couldn't find any pattern in the basic facts presented to him by Dr. Baker. Some patients lived in the country, others in the town of West Branch. He noted something interesting, however: Many patients were teenagers, and, strangely, most of them were boys!

Dr. Schoenbaum met with the five West Branch doctors and did hospital rounds to see their patients. He visited schools in the area. Both the public school and the Catholic school were near each other and only a block away from the main street of the business district. After the rounds Schoenbaum and Baker went back to her office. Dr. Baker had to continue with her critical inoculation program, so she introduced Schoenbaum to James Hasty, the district sanitarian who would act as a local guide when Schoenbaum made the rounds of the homebound patients in the area.

Hasty and Schoenbaum went over the list of patients that Dr. Baker had organized. Schoenbaum noticed one family had as many as six people ill. The doctor thought that six was a lot of people and that he should start his investigation in that very house. As he discovered later, it was the perfect place to start, for this was a house with twins, and only one twin had caught hepatitis.

"If I had only known the exact questions to ask," Dr. Schoenbaum recalls many years later, "I might have solved the case right then and there! But then nobody knows the exact questions to ask until a pattern is found."

This large family of eight, (whom we shall call the Duncans) lived on the outskirts of West Branch. The mother and five of the children were sick with hepatitis. The father and one of the twin boys were well.

Dr. Schoenbaum's first questions were standard ones for an epidemic investigator. Where does your water come from? The Duncans told him it came from their own well. He took a sample for laboratory testing. Where do you buy your milk? They named several stores and the A & P, all in West Branch. They also did all their marketing in these same stores. Do you eat out? They named two drive-in Dairy Queens and the West Branch Bakery where they sometimes purchased baked goods. Have you been to any large gathering lately? They said they hadn't. They also told him this was their only illness in recent years.

Now Dr. Schoenbaum wanted to know the approximate dates the illnesses had started. When did the symptoms appear? Because the incubation for hepatitis A takes between fifteen to fifty days, but takes an average of about thirty days to show up, the doctor knew that the date they became sick minus about thirty days would give him the approximate day of exposure to the virus. All he had to do was count backward by a month, and he knew he would know the general time of the *first contact* with the disease.

This contact date is important. The epidemic hunter uses this date to help patients build a memory calendar. With a special date in mind, people begin to remember what they were doing. Dr. Schoenbaum had them write down or talk aloud and say "This is what I think I did on that day," "Oh, yes, I remember I ate here and here that day," "I visited so and so for lunch," or "I ate in that restaurant." These kinds of memories are essential in tracking an epidemic.

The Duncans took out their calendars and worked backward. The mother and the children became ill on different days. This didn't necessarily mean they didn't have the same source of infection. More likely it indicated the different immunities of each person in the family. The five children and the mother became ill on May 3, 4, 5, and 9. Thirty days earlier meant the epidemic began in early April.

Hasty and Dr. Schoenbaum interviewed four other patients that day. One eleven-year-old boy became sick on May 5, the same day as two of the Duncan boys. This family shopped and ate at exactly the same places as the Duncan family. One thing was different — they had another source of water. This family used town water, not well water. Schoenbaum also interviewed a young mother and her daughter, and a thirty-year-old man who traveled in and out of the town for work. They also used the municipal water and shopped at the same stores and the two Dairy Queens. The mother and daughter went to the West Branch Bakery, but the man said he NEVER went there. He told the doctor about his fight with the owner of the bakery and said he would never set foot in the bakery again. Schoenbaum thought that seemed to eliminate the bakery as a possible source.

Because the community was evenly divided between well water and municipal water, Schoenbaum decided he could cross off water as the source of the infection. He talked to Hasty about milk. Did it come from local dairies? "No," James Hasty told him. "West Branch milk comes from outside the county." Schoenbaum dropped milk from his list of suspected agents.

What about the bakery? The West Branch Bakery? Dr. Schoenbaum sat with pencil poised to cross the bakery off his list. After all, the man with the hepatitis never went into the place, so how could the bakery be a source for the infection? At this point Dr. Schoenbaum was particularly glad that he had a local advisor. "Don't take the bakery off the list," said James Hasty. This same bakery, the West Branch Bakery, actually supplied pastries and bread for most of the markets and restaurants in town. The bakery was left on the list of places to investigate.

Daily, Schoenbaum was in touch with the Centers for Disease Control. He explained that more cases were cropping up. His boss, Dr. Michael Gregg, decided to send in another epidemic intelligence officer to help. James Gardner was finished with his assignment elsewhere in Michigan and had a few days available before his next assignment, in California. Schoenbaum was glad for the skilled help because there were eight new cases. On Wednesday there were four more patients, and by Thursday there were an additional six cases. It would have taken Schoenbaum about two weeks to check all the cases on his own. With Gardner's help they interviewed all fifty-seven cases within a few days.

As Schoenbaum and Gardner talked to people they began to realize that the epidemic reached farther than just West Branch and its county. People told them of friends and relatives who lived far away, people who had visited West Branch and now were sick with hepatitis. Dr. Schoenbaum then learned something very useful. He tracked down at least two earlier cases of hepatitis in West Branch. The jobs of the two people stricken were particularly interesting for an epidemic detective. They were both *food handlers*!

One was a girl who worked at one of the two Dairy Queen drive-ins. The other was a baker at the West Branch Bakery. Both were sick in the early part of April — that meant the timing was right to have infected all the patients in the outbreak. More important, both handled food that was for public consumption. Either one could be the index case, the source of the infection. If they didn't thoroughly wash their hands every time they went to the bathroom and had handled food afterward, they might have passed the infection on at that time.

Schoenbaum was particularly interested in the Dairy Queen worker because a few years before there had been a similar hepatitis epidemic in a rural area in New Jersey. He recalled that the New Jersey cases were all traced to a tainted strawberry sauce in an ice-cream drive-in.

Suspicions were one thing, facts another. Dr. Schoenbaum wanted to visit one of the many patients who were outside of West Branch — someone who had visited, or passed through, the town. There were several choices. Schoenbaum chose the name of a woman who lived thirty miles away in Saginaw Bay. He hoped that an interview with her could pinpoint the cause of her infection.

Dr. Baker took a break from her inoculation program and went with Gardner and Schoenbaum. Schoenbaum recalls how helpful Dr. Baker was in getting the woman, a teacher, to relax and remember all the facts.

The teacher, who will be called Miss Cook, had an excellent memory. She had absolute recall of two visits to West Branch — both in the last three months. She told Schoenbaum the exact date of her first visit: March 20. At that time she had stopped for a cup of coffee. She remembered it because it was the day after her mother's funeral. Her second visit was April 5 on her way to see her dad. She recalled being hungry. She stopped at the West Branch Bakery for a cup of coffee and pastry. The pastry included a piece of coffee cake and three cupcakes with icing. It was a week or so before Easter — the icing was a bright yellow color.

Schoenbaum felt a rush of excitement. This was a key piece of the jigsaw puzzle! Here was a patient with only one brief contact in West Branch — and she had purchased cakes, some with icing. *It had to be the West Branch Bakery!*

But what was it about the bakery? What was it about the way they made baked goods that would pass on an infection? By this time fewer and fewer cases were being reported, and the epidemic had leveled off. But Schoenbaum knew the important thing was to prevent any epidemics in the future.

It was then they learned that the girl from the Dairy Queen couldn't be the index case, after all. There were two Dairy Queens. The one the girl worked in was not the popular place right in town, but one several miles away. Schoenbaum dropped her as a suspect and concentrated on the man from the bakery.

The CDC sent in a replacement for Dr. Gardner: Dr. E. Eugene Page, Jr., from Tennessee. Dr. Schoenbaum and Dr. Page went over the collection of information and the cases, and they made an appointment to visit the bakery. Dr. Schoenbaum carefully explained to the owner that one of the bakers had had hepatitis and might be the central cause of the entire West Branch epidemic. There was no longer any danger in his passing on the virus. The idea now was to find out *why and how* the epidemic had occurred, and how to prevent another one from happening in the future.

The bakery owner was completely helpful. Like everyone else in West Branch, he wanted to limit any spread of the hepatitis. The owner invited the two doctors to visit the bakery anytime after midnight. All the baking was done then, six nights a week. There was a head baker and another man whom we will call Stanley Hope. Hope was the man who had had the hepatitis in early April.

Schoenbaum and Page stood quietly in a corner and watched the two bakers work. There were two kinds of dough—bread and pastry. Schoenbaum exchanged surprised glances with Page when they saw that at every stage of mixing, kneading, and shaping the two bakers *did everything by hand!* That was promising clue. However, they baked the goods at 350° for about a half hour. Schoenbaum knew that the virus of infectious hepatitis was destroyed at half that temperature. So this wasn't the cause. Three hours went by without another clue. At 3:30 A.M. the two bakers took out the icing and glazing materials.

Schoenbaum noticed that they used some frosting from days before, and some of it didn't need any cooking. This sparked his attention. No cooking? Both he and Page watched the process intently. The bakers used their hands to apply both the glaze and the icing. Hope never bothered to use any icing tubes. Instead he squished all the icing through his fingers onto the doughnuts. Hope was so good it was a pleasure to see him work. At the same time it was a hair-raising experience for Schoenbaum.

Hope was a sweet-natured, funny-looking man, who didn't appear to be too bright. It was obvious that he wasn't washing his hands before he glazed and iced everything *by hand*! He had had hepatitis at just the right time in April, and he had every chance to contaminate the icing. The icing wasn't cooked, and it went onto lots of cakes and donuts. If he had contaminated any of the icing, it just stayed contaminated!

Because glazes and icings were held over from day to day, and even used to start new batches, one contaminated batch could account for the fact many people were being contaminated over a *series* of days.

With Hope's poor record of hand washing, it was possible he had contaminated his first batch even before he *felt* sick, since the time of the contagion is just before, and for two weeks after, one feels sick and the skin turns yellow or jaundiced.

Most disease detectives would have thought this proof enough — but not Schoenbaum — and that is why this case is used by every student learning to be a medical detective. Dr. Schoenbaum decided he would have to interview all his cases again. He wanted to find out if his patients had actually eaten the yellow icing, or other glazed pastry or donuts around the day they became ill. April 5 was the target date, as it was the day that Miss Cook had come to town and eaten her yellow glazed cakes.

One by one they interviewed each patient again. Now each patient remembered eating a glazed cake or doughnut. At this time the doctors also solved the mystery of why there were so many *teenage boys* with viral hepatitis. In West Branch most of the boys came into the bakery either at lunchtime or after school. The younger children ate lunch in school.

And what was the Duncan story? How was it one twin did not have the infection? Dr. Schoenbaum went to visit Mrs. Duncan again. Finally he had the right questions to ask! She remembered that on the morning of Friday, April 6, she had gone marketing, and stopped at the bakery on the way home. What had she picked up there? All sorts of iced cupcakes and glazed donuts.

Dr. Schoenbaum asked her how she remembered the date. She remembered it because that day she was rushing back to watch television because Martin Luther King, Jr., had been assassinated on Thursday the night before, and she was anxious to see the news of the riots. She and her two daughters had sat in front of the television set and each of them had eaten a glazed cupcake.

Then the two older boys came in and they ate some pastry. One of them must have eaten more than one doughnut because when the twelve-year-old twins came back from school there was only one glazed doughnut left.

That almost caused a fight when the twin nearest to the pastry grabbed the doughnut and ate it. The other twin was mad, but there was nothing he could do about it. Later on he was glad — because the boy who *didn't* eat the doughnut was the only child in the family who didn't get sick. Mystery solved.

# *The Hunt for the Baffling Bacteria*

*In 1976 there was a raging epidemic. To discover its cause, the state of Pennsylvania and the United States government sent in teams of doctors. Two million dollars and ninety thousand investigative hours later there were still no answers.*

*A lone scientist decided to review his slides one more time. If the small bacteria he was seeking existed, they would show up as a red stain on his slides. Trained microbiologists usually need only a five-minute glance at slides to identify cells they are looking for. He didn't know why he did it, and even though it would be like looking for a grain of rice in a football field, the doctor divided his first slide into grids no larger than a pinprick. With the help of a powerful electron microscope he enlarged the first grid. He saw a flash of red. He didn't know it at first, but that was the first sighting of a new bacterium, one that had never been seen before.*

Ten thousand ex-vets and their families had celebrated the United States bicentennial in Philadelphia. Three days later, many members of the Pennsylvania American Legion came down with a mysterious illness. The news spread like wildfire.

Soon the state, the nation, and the world knew there was a raging epidemic of an unknown disease. Remarkably, if this outbreak had *not* happened to a group of people from the *same* state — people who stayed connected through their small-town roots — probably no one would have heard about the epidemic.

This is how the hunt for the baffling bacteria unfolded.

The legionnaires left the convention on Saturday, July 24, 1976. By Tuesday, the twenty-seventh, many of those who would become sick had already started to feel rotten. In the village of Williamstown, several young American Legion members became very ill and were hospitalized. Tragically, on Sunday, August 1, Korean War veteran James T. Dolen died. The very next day, his friend J.B. died. John B. Ralph, Jr. and Dolen were both members of the same American Legion Post 239. After the autopsy, the doctor described J.B.'s lungs as looking like "Brillo pads." He told J.B.'s aunt that he had never seen anything like it.

Everyone in the 1500-person village of Williamstown seemed to know these two popular Korean

War vets. The entire village, as well as Legion members from nearby towns, turned up for their funerals. It was shocking to go to funerals for such young men. Only a week before people had remembered them as happy and laughing. The shock soon turned into fear.

On that first Tuesday, another of the first victims, forty-seven-year-old Thomas Payne of Chambersberg, Pennsylvania, felt too "fluey" to work. On Wednesday he casually dropped in to see his family doctor. That would turn out to be a good decision. Dr. Stuart Dittmar decided to put Payne in the hospital so that he could watch him more carefully.

On the same day, Tuesday, sixty-one-year-old former Air Force Captain Ray Brennan of Towanda, a village one hundred miles from Philadelphia, also felt ill. He had a fever, a splitting headache, a pain in his chest, and trouble breathing. Unfortunately Brennan refused to go to the hospital. However, because he was so sick, and despite his protests, on Friday his friends and family insisted on rushing him to a hospital. Brennan didn't last through Friday night. The suddenness of Brennan's death was horrifying to everyone.

Frank Aveni, sixty years old, of Clearfield, also came down with chills and a high fever. Aveni's illness looked flulike to his doctor, Roger Hughes. Dr. Hughes was stunned and puzzled when Aveni died suddenly on Friday night.

In Lewisburg, another small Pennsylvania town,

Elmer Hafer had the same symptoms and acute breathing problems. His swift and unexpected death on Sunday shocked his friends.

Meanwhile, back in the village of Chambersberg, Dr. Dittmar was trying everything he knew to bring down Payne's temperature. In case the disease was caused by bacteria, Dr. Dittmar pumped Payne full of antibiotics. To bring down the fever he also tried old-fashioned water therapy. He encouraged Payne to drink lots of cool water, and had the nurses sponge Payne down continuously and wrap him in cold, wet blankets. Dr. Dittmar was stumped but wouldn't give up. Despite all his efforts, Payne's temperature still climbed so high it could have been fatal. When his fever climbed to a dangerous 107.4°F Payne felt he was near death. In a delirium he muttered that he could "see the grim reaper cutting grass" at his feet.

Dittmar kept up the antibiotics and sponging all night, and hour by hour he tested Payne's temperature. At 4:00 Sunday morning the doctor breathed his first sigh of relief — Payne's temperature had finally dropped to 100°F. By 8 A.M. Sunday the temperature was 99°F — almost normal.

All these events took place in a very short space of time thoughout the state. Telephones kept ringing as friends and relatives called from town to town describing the strange illness, high fevers, and gasping breaths of the victims. Legionnaires sobbed together when they learned of the tragic, sudden deaths of their friends. How could people be lively and well one day, and die three days later?

The disease had hit so swiftly on the first days from Tuesday to Sunday, that it wasn't until the next Monday, August 2, that Legion officials notified Pennsylvania state officials. Because Legion members are all veterans of the armed services, the first official telephone call was to the Pennsylvania Veterans Administration (PVA). The doctor in charge acted immediately.

By 9:15 A.M., Monday, the PVA's Dr. Sidney Franklin called Dr. Robert Craven at the Centers for Disease Control — America's disease and epidemic FBI —in Atlanta, Georgia, to report the puzzling deaths of some Philadelphia conventiongoers. He reported the facts: The Pennsylvania members of the American Legion had attended a bicentennial convention in mid-July. The headquarters for the convention was the Bellevue Stratford Hotel. There were now eight deaths among the legionnaires. All of the eight had stayed at the Bellevue Stratford. In addition, there were reports of dangerous illnesses from all over the state. Most of the legionnaires or their guests seemed to have pneumonia.

Very soon after this call eight more persons who stayed at this same hotel died. Another person, Jane Palmer, was deathly ill, and she died shortly thereafter. Palmer had not stayed at the hotel and had not even entered it. However, she had stood in front of the hotel in the sweltering July heat to watch friends in the Legion parade on Friday, July 23.

It didn't take long for newspapers, radio, and television reporters to find out about the epidemic. Soon newspapers were calling it the "Philly Killer." Other reporters called it *Legionnaires' disease*, naming it after the Legion members who were sick and dying. This is the name that stuck.

Every local doctor had a theory about the cause of the disease. The newspapers had carried warnings of an expected winter epidemic of swine flu, which had killed millions in the pandemic of 1917. That is why so many doctors thought this outbreak was an early swine flu. Another early guess was viral pneumonia, or perhaps an entirely new form of pneumonia, or even the rare Q fever, a pneumonia caused by a very tiny microorganism named rickettsia. Other doctors were sure it was a strange and terrible fungus gone wild. Still others thought this illness was the often fatal parrot fever. Indeed, several Pennsylvania physicians, including Dr. Gary Lattimer of Allentown, insisted it *had* to be parrot fever. Dr. Lattimer had seven hospitalized legionnaire patients under his care. He pointed out that there was a perfect match between parrot fever and this disease: a delayed start, a high fever, pneumonia, and a high death rate.

All these theories and more had to be investigated by the State Department of Health experts and the federal Centers for Disease Control (CDC).

The CDC sent in a team of three epidemic hunters. Dr. David Fraser headed this group.

The trio included young epidemiologist Dr. Stephen Thacker. It was his first day on the job. The minute he arrived in his new Virginia office he found an urgent message about the epidemic. By dawn the following day he was on his way to Pennsylvania. He carried with him a special prepared three-page list of questions the CDC wanted answered.

Thacker's first stop was the Chambersberg hospital to interview Dr. Stuart Dittmar and his patient, Thomas Payne. Unlike Columbo and other TV trenchcoat detectives, Dr. Thacker did his interviewing in a white hospital gown and yellow mask. The mask was a necessary protection against contagion.

Using the CDC questionnaire, Dr. Thacker asked Payne about everything he had done at the convention, when he had done it, and whom he had seen. Where did he eat at the convention? Where did he stay during the four days? What hospitality suites did he visit? (The larger Legion posts kept groups of rooms in the covention headquarters to entertain members from other posts.) What symptoms did he have at first?

The question "Did you have any contact with pigs?" really puzzled the patient. The CDC was checking out possible connections with the predicted winter swine flu epidemic.

Thacker's routine was the same at each hospital

throughout the state. He first checked in with the administrator, the infectious-disease control nurse, and the attending doctor. He would then personally read the patients' charts, look over the lab work, and then — in his yellow mask and white gown, — interview the patients. In the cases of those who died, Thacker read the lab and autopsy reports, the after-death investigations into the causes of death. Thacker then called all his information into the State Department of Health in Harrisburg, the capital of Pennsylvania.

At the Harrisburg command post, other scientists evaluated the data. They were looking for clues to the cause, or causes, of the epidemic. They were looking for any groups of clues that could be clumped together. In some ways they were trying to "connect the dots" in order to create a final picture.

Other possible causes of the disease included insecticide sprays that had been used by hotel employees, poison in the water, or even deliberate spraying of the legionnaires. They were looking for natural or man-made poisons that could have been accidentally inhaled by the legionnaires. Everything had to be checked. They even checked on a suspect, a strange "glassy eyed man" in a royal-blue suit who had attended several large meetings at the convention. Several people called in with his description and breathlessly described his strange getup: a bag hanging from the inside of his jacket. Attached to this bag was a tube hidden under his sleeve and across his chest. He also carried a rolled-up newspaper partly hidden in his sleeve. Every so often he would point his hand and newspaper at the partying legionnaires and repeat, "It's too late! You won't be saved. The legionnaires are doomed!" Some people believed this bizarre man had sprayed the legionnaires with poison.

By Wednesday, August 4, twenty-two persons had died of Legionnaires' disease. At that time, Dr. Jay Satz, Pennsylvania's top virus expert, told reporters that he was pretty sure the cause of the epidemic was a *virus*. "But it could be a different type, maybe something that no one has ever seen before. Whatever it is, it's one of the most dangerous things in the world. I've never seen anything like it," said Dr. Satz.

Reporters beseiged Dr. David J. Spencer, director of the federal CDC, for answers. At this point he thought it might be a flu virus. He explained that the CDC was also thoroughly investigating a rare airborne fungus — histoplasmosis — as well as pneumonia-causing parrot fever (caused by a bacteria), and Q fever (caused by a rickettsia bacterium). Also under intense investigation were any special poisons that could cause pneumonia.

Two days later, Dr. Spencer admitted they still did not know what the disease was, but they had ruled out many important bacterial causes such as whooping cough, bubonic plague, typhoid fever, choriomeningitis, tularemia, and Lassa fever. The investigators were moving fast. Field investigators ruled out any food-borne or water-source poisoning. They also announced it could *not* be parrot fever. The Allentown doctor, Dr. Gary Lattimer, disagreed. He still strongly believed the disease was parrot fever.

At first there were only three federal epidemic specialists on loan to the state of Pennsylvania. As the death toll mounted, the CDC rushed in almost a dozen epidemic hunters. As time went on there were about 150 state and federal specialists working on the project. Neither Pennsylvania nor the CDC knew this was the beginning of one of the most thorough and important, and possibly one of the most expensive, investigations in modern medical history. When it was all over, two million dollars would be spent. Scientists and epidemiologists would spend 90,000 hours tracking every tiny detail of Legionnaires' disease. They tested against viruses, known bacteria, fungi, pneumonia-causing organisms, parrot fever, Q fever, poisons, and toxins in the air, food, and water.

These scientists were all looking for an unknown item: an X. They were following any clue that could lead them to this X, and they were searching for common links, as well as differences, among the patients. There had to be some reason why some people got ill and died and others didn't get the disease at all. Only four percent of the 10,000 legionnaires and hotel guests became ill. Only one in six cases was fatal. Why was this? They wanted to match up health facts about survivors. They needed to find out if smoking or drinking were important. It would turn out that most of the deaths happened to smokers.

The investigators also wanted to know if the infection could be caused by an insect bite. Although not one of the victims remembered being bitten, that didn't completely eliminate the possibility that an insect had carried a bacterium. Fleas, lice, mites, and ticks all carry disease. Q fever was still a possibility; it is caused by a bacterium carried by a tick. When Q fever is fatal, the lungs of its victims resemble those of bacterial pneumonia victims.

At the very beginning some tough decisions had to be made. A question that worried everyone was whether or not the Bellevue Stratford was safe for the *next* convention, the Eucharistic Congress. President Gerald Ford was expected to speak at this convention. Should it be held? Would the President of the United States of America be safe addressing the assembly as planned?

Despite a feeling of dread, the Eucharistic Congress went ahead with its meeting in the Bellevue Stratford. Later, Eucharistic Congress and state officials would have reason to regret this decision. Nine of the people who attended the congress later died of Legionnaires' disease. One was a fifty-four-year-old priest, another a thirty-eight-year-old musician.

It was scorchingly hot in July of 1976. The air conditioners in every motel and hotel ran at full blast. Many of the recovering patients recalled seeing a strange "mist" rising from their hotel air conditioners. Others remembered there were annoying damp spots on the carpet in the hotel. CDC investigators took samples from key air conditioners, filters, carpets, and wallpaper to test for any poisonous substances.

They also double-checked ice and ice machines, and restaurants visited by legionnaires and other victims. In case the source of infection came from alcohol, each sick person was asked how much liquor he or she had drunk, what brands were used, and where the alcohol had been purchased or served. One perplexing clue was that most of the victims were men. What bacteria fungus or virus skips over women and attacks only men? The medical detectives didn't know of any. Another tantalizing clue was that most of those who died were smokers. Because of this, CDC epidemiologists checked which brands of cigarettes had been smoked, and where they had been purchased.

All these investigations into the air conditioners, carpets, curtains, alcohol, and cigarettes proved to be fruitless. At this point the only promising lead was the link with the Bellevue Stratford Hotel. One hundred eighty-two patients had either lived at the Bellevue Stratford Hotel, or visited it during the convention. A surprising number of the victims had visited the fourteenth floor hospitality suite. BUT (in science the best of leads sometimes has a *but*), there was also a separate group of thirty-five Legionnaires' disease patients who had *never* had anything to do with the hotel. They had never even entered the hotel.

This last fact puzzled the investigators. Did that mean there were two separate epidemics? Just in case there were two epidemics, the investigation was divided into two parts: Legionnaires' disease and Broad Street pneumonia. Broad Street is a street in Philadelphia.

Hundreds of reporters came from all over the world. Every day TV commentators reported on the disease-related events throughout Pennsylvania. Fortunately it didn't take long for the investigators to decide this often fatal disease was not the flu and was *not contagious*.

They felt it wasn't contagious because only a small percentage of the legionnaires came down with the disease. Besides, there was key information on the hotel employees. Aside from one hotel employee who had died, no other employees had called in sick during or after, the epidemic. If Legionnaires' disease were contagious, more hotel employees would have been victims.

The mystery kept on deepening. The CDC sent more investigators to Pennsylvania, which meant there were twenty epidemic intelligence officers — about one fourth the total in the whole of the United States — looking into the causes of Legionnaires' disease. There were also about 100 state health department investigators working on the case. Dr. William Perkin headed the state teams.

The fear of catching Legionnaires' disease, and the terrifying news of the nine deaths from the Eucharistic Congress, kept many future conventions away from Philadelphia that summer. Two groups, Girls Nation and the American Legion's Boys cancelled plans to visit the city in August.

On the other hand, the national publicity about Legionnaires' disease did one good thing: It uncovered other mysterious deaths that had occurred *before* the legionnaires' meeting. Early in July, Philadelphia had been host to several conventions, including those for magicians and for candle makers. After scattering to their homes in other parts of the country, two magicians and one candle maker had died of pneumonia. Since pneumonia is a rather common form of death, no one had connected their illnesses to an earlier visit to Philadelphia. However, because everyone was now alerted to the impact of Legionnaires' disease, when the nine members of the Eucharistic Congress died after the legionnaires did, everyone knew it was an ongoing part of the epidemic. Did the fact that candle makers and magicians had also died in the preceding week provide a link of some kind? This was a significant question that had to be answered. For instance, if there had been other outbreaks, where and when had they happened? And were there any unsolved cases locked in the CDC vault that matched those of Legionnaires' disease?

Despite their exhaustive work and the vast data the state and the CDC had gathered, they were all stumped. What was the cause of the epidemic? How did it spread? In every laboratory of the State Department of Health, in every special disease building of the Centers for Disease Control in Atlanta, microbiologists were working to identify the organism that caused this disease.

Q fever, which is caused by a rod-shaped organism called rickettsia, was one of the important target diseases that had to be ruled out. In Atlanta, Georgia, all CDC investigations on Q fever took place within the high-security confines of Building Seven, which houses the leprosy and rickettsia lab. In the absence of its director, Dr. Charles Shepard, who was on a backpacking trip in Wyoming, the investigation was being conducted by microbiologist Dr. Joseph McDade.

All through that difficult, hot summer, McDade searched for a link between Q fever and Legionnaires' disease. Day after day he inoculated guinea pigs with material from the lungs of persons who had died in the recent epidemic. If it was Q fever, these guinea pigs would become ill with fevers and die. After death, the guinea-pig tissues were put on slides and stained with a special red dye that would tint any rickettsia organisms. McDade could then easily detect the rod-shaped bacteria under his powerful microscope.

Even though some of the animals did become ill and die, McDade could not find any of the rod-shaped germs in their tissues. Legionnaires' disease did not appear to be caused by rickettsia. Dead end!

In other laboratories, other infectious disease specialists arrived at the same dead end. Each, in turn, ruled out fungi, bacteria, and various viruses as possible sources of the epidemic.

Because so many known diseases had been ruled out, most of the search now concentrated on poisonous chemicals. These chemicals ranged from pesticides to industrial chemicals. Again researchers hit a frustrating blind alley.

If the CDC experts couldn't identify the cause of Legionnaires' disease, that didn't stop ordinary (and some crazy) people from forming their own odd conclusions.

There were people who just *knew* it was the man in the royal-blue suit — the man with the tube that he kept on pointing at legionnaires. There was a man who called the CDC to say it was contaminated soda — that he had such a can and it was filled with viral pneumonia bacteria. Then there were the outer-space believers. One minister thought Legionnaires' was a disease from outer space. Many other people called to say it had to be a Martian payback. They explained the Martians were mad because the *Viking I* spacecraft had landed on Mars in July. The Philadelphia Department of Health received a long letter from a man named Jackson. The letter insisted that the singer Frank Sinatra was the cause of the epidemic!

Since they had no answers as yet from their own CDC experts, in late August, the Centers for Disease Control called an extraordinary conference of twelve of the nation's top pathologists, experts in recognizing healthy and diseased tissues under a microscope. Each of these laboratory experts was invited to examine, separately and together, every known detail about Legionnaires' disease. Each doctor examined key tissue and blood sample slides, and reviewed all the collected test information.

These twelve experts came to these conclusions: Legionnaires' disease could not be caused by:

1. a toxic chemical
2. a virus
3. a bacterium.

So what was it? None of the world's leading pathologists knew. It was frustrating. The best scientific minds in the country had examined every aspect of the epidemic but could find nothing. Scientists everywhere shook their heads in disbelief.

It now appeared that despite the enormous resources and work put in, Legionnaires' disease would be an unsolved mystery. Most of the tissue samples and blood samples would be sent to a special freezer to be stored with other evidence of unexplained epidemics.

By December the chances of finding the answers looked bleak. The head of the epidemiology team at CDC, Dr. David Fraser, prepared his epidemic progress investigation report. It was delivered to each laboratory immediately after Christmas. Dr. Fraser personally brought a copy to his old friend, Dr. Shepard, in Building Seven.

When Dr. Joseph McDade came back to work in Building Seven two days after Christmas, the first thing he did was read the Fraser EPI-2 report. One thing in the report surprised him. It seemed Q fever had *not* yet been ruled out. That meant that Legionnaires' disease might still be caused by rickettsia, a microorganism that was his specialty.

Dr. McDade sat there thinking about that possibility. When he had done his overview of the tissue slides (they were slides of guinea pigs injected with the lung tissues of dead legionnaires), there had not been any trace of the rod-shaped rickettsia.

But the progress report made Dr. McDade think. What if he hadn't recognized "it" because this disease was an entirely new form of rickettsia? It had been at least fifty years since any scientist had identified a new form. With great excitement Dr. McDade picked up the box of the four-month-old slides. Fortunately all the slides were stained in a special way. Bacteria or rickettsia would show up red.

Dr. McDade decided on a new approach. Last

summer he had done five-minute overviews of each slide. Five minutes is all a trained microbiologist usually needs to identify organisms. He had not seen any red-stained rickettsia. This time, instead of doing a quick overall study of each slide, Dr. McDade decided — he doesn't remember why — on a speck-by-speck, millimeter-by-millimeter search.

The powerful electron microscopes of the CDC not only magnify tissue, they can divide each millimeter of a sample to make a grid. This makes it easier to find things later. Dr. McDade worked carefully. After all, each area he would magnify was no bigger than a *pinprick*.

Bingo! In the cells of an infected guinea pig he could see a tiny, very, very tiny red speck. A small cluster of red *rods*. Rickettsia are rod-shaped. But these rods were too big to be rickettsia. Could they be bacteria? He immediately shared his discovery with his director, Dr. Shepard, who was a world authority on rickettsia organisms.

The two scientists decided to pursue this unexpected tiny clue together. Each doctor took small samples from the original frozen tissues. Each sample had been carefully labeled and preserved after the original slide had been prepared months earlier. McDade and Shepard inoculated these samples into fertilized eggs.

Back in August this same laboratory group had tried to grow the rickettsia the same way. However, in the summer all the eggs had been treated with antibiotics. This was to prevent contamination from common bacteria. Now McDade ordered eggs from chickens that had never received antibiotics. He decided not to add any antibiotics to the tissues, either. This would turn out to be a brilliant decision. McDade injected the first tissues on New Year's Eve.

Five days later, Wednesday, January 5, 1977, the embryos in the eggs began to die. Since bacteria would have killed them in two days, McDade and Shepard thought they might have an unusual — maybe new — form of rickettsia on their hands. McDade removed fluid from the egg. He stained it red and eagerly peered at this new slide under his microscope.

*The slide was flooded with rod-shaped organisms.*

What happened next was puzzling. The rods were definitely too big to be rickettsia. But they certainly didn't look like any bacteria they had ever seen in a laboratory. And, unlike most bacteria, these organisms couldn't grow on any of the usual nutrients. This was frustrating!

What the doctors still didn't know was whether the rods had any connection with Legionnaires' disease. But they knew the only way to find the answer was to obtain blood from recovered Legionnaires' disease victims. Their next step was an antibody test.

Whenever a person survives a disease, his or her blood contains antibodies. Anytime you have a cold virus, or an infection, or chicken pox, your body reacts to the strange substance in your body. This strange substance, whether it be a virus, a bacteria, a bacterial toxin, or a foreign protein, is called an antigen. The reaction to the antigen is called an *antibody*. Antibodies of various types give immunity and help neutralize the antigen. Anyone who had recovered from Legionnaires' disease would have antibodies to the disease.

Anything to do with Legionnaires' disease was hot news. But until McDade and Shepard were certain of their findings it was important to keep the exciting observations to themselves. That is why Dr. Shepard did not go through general channels for the blood, but instead quietly made the request to a fellow CDC scientist. He got samples of blood from five *recovered* Legionnaires' disease victims.

The two microbiologists knew they had to stain the antibodies with a fluorescent dye. Under the light from a special microscope the telltale antibodies would glow yellow-green. This procedure is called a fluorescent antibody test. *If* the disease that the legionnaires had suffered was caused by McDade's rods, the antibodies in the recovered legionnaire's blood would connect the rods to the fluorescent antibody and glow.

Martha Redus was the CDC expert on fluorescent antibodies. They called on her expertise. She painstakingly added the stains. She had to allow time for the fluorescent antibodies to attach. She washed the slide free of contaminating substances and dried it. The slides would take some time to be ready. Joe McDade, already exhausted from nonstop investigation, went home to sleep.

This was Friday, January 7. At 8 P.M. McDade's telephone rang. Martha Redus was excited. Two of the five serum samples from recovering legionnaires had connected to the rods! This was extremely important and exciting news. Later they would discover why only two samples had responded to the injection. Most people — especially if they weren't healthy to begin with — did not immediately create antibodies to Legionnaires' disease. Many patients took as long as six weeks. That explained why three of the samples didn't attach to rods. They were taken too early in the illness.

If two of the samples reacted, the scientists knew they had discovered a bacterialike germ that had been the cause of the Philadelphia outbreak! What about the other samples that had been labeled Broad Street pneumonia? McDade tested them, too. YES! They also reacted to the rods. So Broad Street pneumonia and Legionnaires' disease were one and the same.

How could they be absolutely sure about their discovery? There had been so many false starts and announcements with Legionnaires' disease that Drs. Shepard and McDade still wanted to hold back the news. They needed more blood to test. But blood samples from recovered Legionnaires' disease victims were extremely rare. Could they get more? They explained their need to the scientist in charge of the frozen blood samples. He rushed a new supply to them. The additional tests confirmed their discovery.

Another set of mysteries could now be unraveled. For a long time Dr. Shepard had thought Legionnaires' disease acted in a similar way to a fatal epidemic at St. Elizabeth's Hospital in Washington, D.C., several years before. Also in the CDC unsolved mystery vaults were tissues and blood samples from yet another tragic epidemic that had occurred a long time ago in Pontiac, Michigan.

Dr. Shepard took all these samples and injected them with the newly discovered rods. Both the Pontiac fever and the St. Elizabeth's epidemic matched with Legionnaires' disease. This was fantastic news. Two older medical mysteries were now solved.

McDade and Shepard had confirmed their theories with facts. The country could be informed.

January 18, 1977, five months after the epidemic, the Centers for Disease Control announced they had discovered a new bacterium. It was not only responsible for Legionnaires' disease but for many other epidemics as well. The official name was *Legionella pneumonophilia*: lung-loving legion.

But the scientists' job wasn't over quite yet. How did Legionnaires' disease actually spread? Where did the bacterium come from? What was the best way to treat the disease? Was there any way to prevent the disease?

What they discovered was astonishing. Legionnaires' disease was actually an ancient disease! The tiny, tiny bacteria could be found all over the world! It exists everywhere.

The disease is not spread from person to person. You cannot catch it from another human being. How then is this infection spread? Legionnaires' disease usually is spread through water-mist machines. It is spread often through cooling systems on top of buildings. If these systems are not disinfected and cleaned, they can spread the infection through particles of water. Any aerosol-producing device such as cooling towers, whirlpool baths, showers, and respiratory equipment can spread the disease. Mostly this has happened in hospitals or hotels, but a 1990 epidemic was traced to a water-misting machine in the vegetable department of a supermarket. The machine had not been cleaned thoroughly enough. New standards were set for these machines.

In 1991 there was an outbreak among toll takers and guards in an underwater tunnel between New Jersey and New York.

The more the scientists investigated the bacterium, the more they found that antibodies to it can be found in a great many healthy people's blood. This fact solved the mystery of why so few of the hotel staff called in sick during the height of the epidemic in July and August 1976. Most of the staff had already caught mild cases of Legionnaires' disease. At the time of his or her illness each person probably thought he or she had a mild flu. When anyone catches a disease and recovers from it, that individual carries antibodies to the bacterium. That person is then immune to the disease and can't catch it again.

The investigators discovered that Legionnaires' disease can cause either a light outbreak or a fatal one. How badly it affects a person depends on how healthy he or she is at that time. All those who died in the Philadelphia epidemic were heavy smokers. Their lung tissues were not healthy enough to fight against this "lung-loving" disease.

# *Unraveling a Riddle*

*It was a steamy summer night in Jackson, Mississippi. The slender doctor looked up from his charts. He could hear a boy's voice whispering, "Don't wake anyone up!" The doctor smiled. He turned off his kerosene lamp and, playing a crazy hunch, hid behind his office door. He could see the three twelve-year-old boys whom the orphanage matron called, "our three devils." They were stealing food from the orphanage kitchen!*

*He watched the three boys and found the secret, and his third and final clue to the 200-year-old pellagra puzzle. Dr. Joseph Goldberger was on his way to solving another medical mystery.*

**P**ellagra, a devastating disease whose name means rough skin, occurred every spring in crowded places, particularly in the south. Here people believed that the disease was an infection that was passed from one to another. No one knew why some men, women, or children recovered from pellagra. Patients who did not recover became insane.

Pellagra started with a small rash that looked like a sunburn. It erupted on the face, neck, hands, forearms, and feet. This turned into pimple-like sores that became swollen, red, and hard. When the pimples broke they left a blackened crust. The people with pellagra (pellagrins) had extremely reddened tongues and a burning sensation in their mouths. Pellagra patients felt extremely nervous. In advanced cases patients got severe diarrhea, couldn't sleep, moved in jerks and spasms, (almost as if they were terribly drunk), and showed different stages of insanity. It was a terrible disease.

The odd thing about pellagra, a disease that existed in many European countries, especially in Italy, was that in the United States it mainly existed in the Deep South and attacked poor women, men, and children. After the devastating 1907 floods, the disease multiplied. By 1914 there were *100,000* cases in prisons, orphanages, old-age homes, sanitariums for the insane, and cotton-mill towns.

Many thousands of cotton-mill workers had pellagra, and that meant factories were shorthanded. Two cotton-factory owners were so hampered by the steady loss of workers in their mills that they created the Thompson-McFadden Pellagra Commission to delve into pellagra research. They headed this commission with three doctors who were experts on the disease.

After an exhaustive investigation, these three famous doctors solemnly announced that pellagra was an infection caused by an unknown living microorganism — in other words, a contagious disease caused by bacteria. They found no other way to explain how the epidemic expanded so quickly except to declare it was spread by the stable fly. This fly could be found throughout the South in 1914.

Another expert team, a part of the Public Health Service, had been working on the pellagra riddle for five years. The team went to Italy, where there were hundreds, sometimes thousands of pellagra patients each year. In Italy, the theory at the time was that pellagra was caused by spoiled corn. Although the members of this team tracked down every possible clue, they could not come to any conclusions as to the cause of pellagra. It looked like pellagra would go on for another 200 years before anyone found what caused it.

The Public Health Service began to feel pressure, particularly from people in the South, to find the cause — and a cure. The Surgeon General didn't know quite what to do. A team had worked five years and had found nothing. Should they send in yet another team? The Surgeon General's staff urged General Rupert Blue to send Dr. Joseph Goldberger, one of the elite epidemic fighters in a corps called the Hygienic Laboratory. Years later this group provided the nucleus of epidemic investigators in the famed Centers for Disease Control.

Goldberger was known to be super-smart, cautious, and dedicated. He had shown his scientific genius in many earlier investigations. Further, Assistant Surgeon General J. W. Kerr thought Goldberger had an ability to see things in a fresh and creative way. It was obvious that pellagra needed just such a fresh approach. Kerr's boss, Surgeon General Blue, hesitated to waste Goldberger's time on a no-win pellagra investigation, but Kerr finally persuaded Blue. Goldberger turned out to be an inspired choice.

At first Goldberger was irritable and unhappy about the assignment. It would mean several years of intense traveling throughout the South, which would mean he wouldn't see much of his wife and children. He also knew that pellagra had defeated all previous investigators. Goldberger's friends privately urged him not to take on the assignment. They turned the words *stable fly* into a joke, and told him there was a "fly in the ointment" — meaning something would surely go wrong in any pellagra investigation. Goldberger's fellow disease investigators believed that no one could find the answer to the 200-year-old riddle, and that this assignment would be a dead end for Goldberger's promising Public Health Service career.

But Dr. Goldberger took on the difficult assignment. With an assistant, he traveled by buggy, by the newfangled car, by train, through every part of the South. As Goldberger wandered through the misery spots where pellagra existed, he filled notebook after notebook with his observations, details, and figures.

In each southern town, in the hospitals, in prisons, in old-age homes, and orphan asylums, he observed thousands of sick people. Their faces, hands, and feet were covered with cracked crusts of reddened skin. He saw thousands of mentally disturbed and insane pellagra patients.

In Milledgeville, Georgia, in the Georgia State Sanitarium for the Insane, Goldberger had an odd feeling. But he couldn't quite put his feelings into a solid thought.

He knew it had something to do with the staff of the sanitarium. Was it something anyone had said? No! It was what *no one* had said! It was that none of the 293-person staff of doctors, nurses, or attendants seemed afraid of pellagra.

On the outside, Goldberger knew people were deathly afraid of getting the disease from someone who already had it. Why were the people in this sanitarium indifferent to catching it?

Something else passed through Goldberger's mind, a second thought that overlapped the first. Not only at this sanitarium, but at *all* the hospitals and prisons and homes, the staffs felt the same way! Unlike the average Southerner, the doctors, nurses, and attendants didn't seem to worry about catching pellagra. Why did they think they were immune? He didn't know it yet, but their attitude was clue number one.

Pellagra cases seemed to erupt every springtime. If the disease was spread by an insect, Goldberger asked himself, what insect or bacterium only came out in the spring? And if it was an insect, why didn't it ever attack any staff members?

He puzzled over the fact that the disease could be found much more in the countryside and a lot less in cities. And why did the disease skip over middle class and rich people and mostly attack poor people?

Everyone thought pellagra was contagious. But Goldberger realized he had never heard it mentioned as a disease in either the army or navy. One would think that the close quarters in the armed services would encourage a raging epidemic. This was clue number two.

Something else bothered Goldberger. As he had read and reread his notes about the Methodist Orphan Asylum in Jackson, Mississippi, Goldberger noticed a pattern of illness that did not exist anywhere else in the South. When he reread the notes he thought it just couldn't be true! All the patients at the orphanage were in the same age group. All of them were *between the ages of six and twelve*! Now that was strange. How could any contagious disease just skip over the babies, toddlers, and children under six? And why did pellagra "ignore" orphans over the age of twelve? Goldberger and his assistant, Dr. Clarence Waring, made a special second train trip to Jackson in hopes of finding answers to this mystery. While he didn't realize it, he was on the way to finding clue number three.

In the Methodist Orphanage, Dr. Goldberger had long talks with the stern matron in charge of the home. He asked her all kinds of things about the care of the children. The matron quickly admitted they had a money problem at the home. So it had been the policy at this orphanage to give milk to only the very youngest children. "As far as the oldest children, go, they do the chores, so we have to give them more food. In fact, we give them meat and vegetables at least once a week! Sometimes they also get milk." Then the matron said something that really made Goldberger's ears perk up. "We don't give the youngsters between the ages of six and twelve any milk to drink. It is a policy to not give them any meat or vegetables, either."

Goldberger asked her to repeat what she had just said. The kids from six to twelve were not given vegetables, milk, or meat. Was this the answer to the pellagra puzzle? Was this why only the children between ages six and twelve were sick? But were they all sick?

"Are there any kids in that age bracket who do not have pellagra?" asked Goldberger. "Sure," the matron replied. "There are three twelve-year-old boys — little devils they are, devils who never caught pellagra!" Goldberger wondered why she called the three boys "little devils."

At that moment one of the most respected scientists in the Public Health Service decided to play detective. He watched the three boys day and night. That is how he discovered them stealing food from the orphanage kitchen one midnight. He also watched them steal glasses of milk from the youngest kids. It was unbelievable — they even stole meat from the plates of the older children! *These three boys were eating better than any of the other children in the orphanage.*

What did it all mean? Was it possible that these boys could resist pellagra because they were eating special food? Was it possible the riddle he was trying to unravel didn't have anything to do with infection, but everything to do with *immunity*? Goldberger's idea was getting clearer and clearer.

People who investigate epidemics work with facts, but they also work with their instincts. Now Goldberger's observations on doctors, nurses, matrons, and attendants popped back into his mind. These made him recall his thoughts about the pellagra-free army and navy. Was the whole question of pellagra a question of *food*? As a public health officer, Goldberger knew about the balanced rations in the armed forces. How did that connect with hospital staffs? Of course! The staffs ate separately, and differently, from their charges. Goldberger easily recalled that while the food wasn't great, it usually included some meat, fresh vegetables, and even milk.

These clues were worth investigating. "Let's look

into diet!" Goldberger told Waring. He sent for his other assistant, Willets. The three men soon discovered that the diet for the sick children was exactly the same monotonous high sugar, corn, and hog fat as the diet in the prisons, sanitariums, and old-age homes that had thousands of pellagra patients. This diet was also the diet of the average poor Southerner. The diet consisted mainly of items made of corn: corn biscuits, hominy grits, corn mush, corn syrup, and molasses made of corn, along with some gravy and fat from pigs. *What was missing?* The people on the hospital staffs, the very people who never seemed to get pellegra, ate milk, butter, eggs, or lean meats.

Was it protein that was missing? Or vitamins? Both words were new ones in the recently discovered science of nutrition. In fact, the very word *vitamin* had been invented only three years before, in 1911.

Science is a mixture of creative inspiration and hard work. Goldberger decided on an entirely new approach to the investigation. But in order to back himself up in case his hunches about nutrition were wrong, he also thought of ways to check the infection theory. He arranged to work with Edward Francis, one of the Public Health Service's top laboratory investigators. Together they decided to use monkeys to prove (or disprove) whether the disease could be passed from one person to another.

Now Goldberger would proceed with an extremely daring idea. He would try to *prevent* pellagra next spring.

He would accomplish this with diet. He planned to work with both the neglected orphans and the mentally disturbed in insane asylums.

He approached Surgeon General Blue with a two-year plan: He and his assistants would plan a new diet for the orphans at the Methodist Orphanage and the nearby Baptist Orphanage, which had 130 pellagra patients (and had had pellagra patients every spring since its opening in 1897). Goldberger wanted to try out his food theory that the army garrison ration, the navy ration, and the Phillippine Scout ration could actually keep people from "catching" pellagra. He was hoping that if his food theories were correct, he could prevent any more of the orphans from getting pellagra next spring.

The test started in September 1914. Every child under six received twenty-one ounces of milk a day. Those over twelve years got fourteen ounces of milk a day. Up until this point, the children hadn't been given eggs. Now they had eggs every day. Fresh meat was to be served four days a week, instead of once a week.

The test didn't need two years. In only a few *weeks* the food acted like a magic paintbrush — pellagra seemed to just fade away. The children come out of their pellagra stupor and started to bloom again.

Public Health Service officials in Washington

urged Goldberger to publish the results, but, ever cautious and careful, he didn't rush off with the news. He decided to wait until the following spring to see if the diet would prevent new cases of pellagra.

Goldberger started a similar program for the patients in the Georgia State Sanitarium for the Insane. One white ward and one black ward were given the same food as the orphans. Two other control groups were given the old corn-rich diet. Willets stayed at the asylum, and Waring stayed at the orphanage. Goldberger traveled between these two places in Georgia and Mississippi, as well as to other homes and mill towns filled with pellagra patients.

Everyone waited for the results in the spring. Would the Methodist Orphanage have the anticipated yearly increase of thirty-three new cases? Would the Baptist home have the expected fifty-two new cases?

The results were astounding! There were *no* new cases that spring! Food *could* cure and banish pellagra!

This news was so amazing *The New York Times* carried this headline:

PELLAGRA NOT CONTAGIOUS
CAUSED BY IMPROPER DIET
DECLARES PUBLIC HEALTH DOCTOR

Congratulations came in from experts from all

over the world — everywhere but in the American South. Medical personnel divided into two camps. All Public Health officials and most other leading research scientists accepted Goldberger's well-documented conclusions about the effect of diet. But many Southern politicians and doctors opposed the diet theory with great energy, attacking Goldberger at medical meetings and in the local press as if he were a liar and a thief!

"Pellegra has to be infectious!" said these opponents. There were many public meetings and countless newspaper stories denouncing the Public Health Service and Goldberger as fools.

The worst attacks came from the Thompson-McFadden Pellagra Commission's three pellagra experts. They scoffed at Goldberger and his results and even tried to discredit him. At endless meetings, these doctors claimed they had investigated and discarded the idea of faulty diet! "There is no connection between pellagra and diet," they declared. Most of the Southern press ran their stories again and again.

Everyone was discouraged by the attacks. Everyone but Goldberger. "We just have to be missionaries," he said. "Food missionaries."

Goldberger decided that he *had* to think of another daring idea. He had satisfactorily proved he could *erase* pellagra with proper diet, but now that these findings were under attack, he would have to prove he could *cause* pellagra with faulty diet.

Goldberger had the whole plan in his head, but

his first problem was to find a safe, *secret*, clean place where he could conduct a controlled experiment on at least twelve healthy volunteers for six months. He would also need a large group of people who were on a natural diet, but living under the same circumstances.

But what could he offer these people? It was then that he thought of prison inmates. Inmates had something to gain. They would be given their freedom at the end of the experiment.

Goldberger had a fan in Mississippi, a Dr. E. H. Galloway of the State Department of Health. Goldberger confided his plan to Galloway, who enthusiastically offered to talk to Governor Earl Brewer. It was a daring idea, but a delicate one. What if any of the volunteers died? What if there were legal restrictions? What would the public think of such a risky plan, especially since they were so afraid of pellagra themselves?

Goldberger met with Governor Brewer and worked out every problem. He asked for a corner of a model prison farm, and said the United States government would build clean, screened-in barracks with sinks (the men would have to be ultra-clean, and not have the possibility of insect bites).

"Can you help us to get twelve healthy white volunteers?" asked Goldberger. He explained that it was thought that white males had a harder time catching pellagra than did black males. If he could produce pellagra in these men, it would make his case stronger.

"Twelve white men," Governor Brewer agreed. "But you can't have these convicts one day longer than six months! After that I'm going to pardon them whether or not they have your disease!"

Goldberger explained that the six-month diet would consist of grits, syrup, mush, biscuits, corn bread, cabbage, sweet potatoes, rice, collards, and coffee with sugar but not milk. The men would be allowed any amount of this food they desired — but they couldn't eat anything else for the six months.

The prison volunteers were murderers, burglars, forgers, and embezzlers. Fortunately, Goldberger found an able and bully-proof scientist, Dr. G. Wheeler, to supervise the experiment. Wheeler also supervised a control group of eighty working convicts who also lived in the new wing with the clean, screened-in barracks. However, these men had a separate kitchen and would be fed only *fresh foods*.

The barracks were opened on April 19. The twelve volunteer prisoners loved the diet. They could eat all they wanted, and the food was tasty. All they had to do for six months was eat and then go free??? What a bargain!

The men began the experiment with high spirits and jokes. Within a few weeks they started fighting with each other and became mean and suspicious. One by one the volunteers started to complain about burning mouths and reddened tongues.

Most had headaches. Others had backaches, stomachaches, or were dizzy. One man who turned out to have a serious illness was dismissed from the project. This left eleven men.

Wheeler checked the eleven men every day. Goldberger was at the Jackson prison farm often and checked them, too. Week after week, month after month they checked the men. So far nothing! There were no pellagra rashes. April, May, June, July, August passed. It was true the men looked awful and couldn't work anymore. The formerly happy-go-lucky men were crabby and irritable. Was it possible there were two forms of pellagra? Or was this the early stage of the disease?

One thing was certain, the men all hated the diet. They begged for some meat. Goldberger allowed them a little.

During all this time Goldberger was running back and forth between one city and another in the South. Not only was he supervising laboratory experiments to induce pellagra in monkeys, he had forced himself to become a "feed-bag" missionary. His personal mission was to improve the diet in every institution in the South. He presented his early results in the sanitarium and the orphanages. He was dumbfounded when he met with resistance. He was up against budget-minded officials. But worst of all, these same officials had closed minds. They did not believe that diet had anything to do with pellagra. They *wanted* to believe, and were therefore totally convinced, that pellagra was a contagious disease.

September rolled around. Goldberger and Wheeler were worried. Was six months long enough? Probably not. But they couldn't keep the men one day past six months. At this point the usually optimistic Wheeler was depressed and thought the experiment would turn out to be a failure. But just one month before the deadline Wheeler *found a rash on one man*! He wired Goldberger to hurry back to Jackson.

"We've done it!" Goldberger said to Wheeler.

By September 24 there were five men with solid pellagra rashes on various parts of their bodies. It was a much higher percentage then Goldberger had dreamed would be possible. "The most I had hoped for, the most I had prayed for was two cases," he said.

To "prove" his case, Goldberger called in two Mississippi experts on the disease. One was Dr. Nolan Stewart, superintendent of the Mississippi State Hospital for the Insane. It was pellagra! Two professors of dermatology, one from Tennessee and one from St. Louis, Missouri, also came to examine the men. There was no doubt. Five volunteers on Goldberger's faulty diet had developed the first hard evidence of pellagra.

All the convicts were given their promised pardons. None stayed to be cured.

The published results created a sensation, and congratulations poured into Goldberger's office and home from all over the world. One prominent scientist wrote that this was one of the most important discoveries in preventive medicine since beriberi, a disease caused by a lack of thiamine, had been discovered. Another wrote that if Goldberger were a citizen of Great Britain he would surely have been knighted for such distinguished services to the nation.

Meanwhile at the lab, Edward Francis conducted painstaking experiments. He could find no way for rhesus monkeys to pass pellagra from one to another. Francis's report ended with this verdict: "We just can't transmit the disease! No monkey can 'catch' pellagra. I've tried everything!"

Because there was still so much opposition in the Southern press; and from Southern doctors and officials, Goldberger dreamed up still another proof. He was so sure that pellagra could not be contagious that he decided to repeat Francis's monkey experiments on *human volunteers*. Goldberger, his wife, Mary, and thirteen scientist friends participated as human guinea pigs. First one healthy volunteer was injected with *blood* from a pellagra patient. The next part of the experiment was even more sickening. In order to prove, once and for all, that no one could "catch" pellagra, Goldberger, his wife, and his friends chewed pills made from nasal secretions, urine, lesions, and feces of pellagra patients. His results — no one caught pellagra of course — were hailed in newspaper articles around the country under the headline FIFTEEN MEN AND A HOUSEWIFE.

It still took years to convince local officials to rethink the pellagra problem. Occasionally Goldberger worked on other projects, but his main effort was to find a cheap food that could be used as a pellagra preventive. His work was aided when they accidentally found out that a local dogs' disease called black tongue was actually the same condition as pellagra. When brewer's yeast cured the dogs, they knew they had found a way to prevent the disease.

Eventually, years later, Goldberger and his men discovered there was actually a vitamin — niacin — missing from pellagra victims' diet. Scientists called the vitamin *vitamin G*, some say for Goldberger, but actually because vitamins are listed alphabetically in the order they are discovered. Later, the British discovered that niacin (nicotinic acid) is chemically part of the vitamin B family. That eliminated it as a separate vitamin G.

Goldberger's hunch on "immunity" helped turn the tide in preventing pellagra. Years later, when pure niacin was finally isolated, it was fed to advanced pellagra patients. They showed enormous improvements within twenty-four hours. Doctors still find evidence of the disease, especially among severe alcoholics and the mentally disturbed. Shots of niacin can cure them. Goldberger was one of the pioneers who proved the relationship of food to good health.

# SCHOLASTIC BIOGRAPHY